Criminalistics for

Spanish↔English

Interpreters

Linda Cutana

Compiled by
Désirée Baker Millikan

Illustrations by
Pedro Pablo Camacho

Published by: Cantemos
               Chino Hills, CA 91709

Library of Congress Control Number: 2010913237
ISBN 1-892306-25-5

Publisher's Cataloging-in-Publication
(Provided by Quality Books, Inc.)

Millikan, Desiree Baker.
    Criminalistics for Spanish-English interpreters / compiled by Desiree Baker Millikan ; illustrations by Pedro Pablo Camacho.
    p. cm.
    Includes bibliographical references.
    LCCN 2010913237
    ISBN-13: 978-1-892306-25-8
    ISBN-10: 1-89230-625-5

    1. Forensic sciences--Translating--Dictionaries. 2. Spanish language--Translating into English--Dictionaries. 3. English language--Translating into Spanish--Dictionaries.   I. Title.

HV8073.M55 2010   363.25
                         QBI10-600188

CONTENTS

PREFACE

Expert witness testimony presents unique challenges for court interpreters, in terms of specialized vocabulary and the speed and complexity of testimony. This compilation of forensic terminology is by no means all-inclusive, nor is it intended as a substitute for specialized dictionaries. Its aim is to facilitate the interpreter's task by bringing together, under one cover, commonly used forensic terms and related vocabulary used in court settings by forensic scientists testifying as expert witnesses. Although, for the most part, "commonly-used" or "well-known" words are not included, this compilation does incorporate frequently uttered nuances, such as "fleck, chip, scraping, shaving, shard, or spatter."

mota/ astilla raspadura viruta fragmento salpicadura
Salp·cadura

The handbook includes an alphabetical listing in English and Spanish. It also includes subject categories, (e.g. trace, ballistics, fingerprints), which are listed alphabetically in English only, since the principal target audience is the interpreter working in the North American criminal court setting. These latter categories include the terms commonly used by criminalists testifying about that particular subject. The aim is to enable the interpreter to turn to that section, if he or she is faced with the task of interpreting for a ballistics expert, for example. In many instances, the categories overlap in certain aspects, so certain vocabulary may appear in more than one subject category. Every word in the subject categories is included in the alphabetical listings in both English and Spanish. The alphabetical listings

Criminalistics for Spanish↔English Interpreters

include vocabulary from other forensic specialties, which I decided did not merit a separate subject category due to their relatively rare occurrence in courtroom testimony.

To keep the handbook to a manageable size, usually only one Spanish or English equivalent has been included, even though there may be more than one way to say any given word.

I hope that my fellow interpreters find this handbook useful. Comments and suggestions are welcome and may be sent to: csimillikan@gmail.com.

DISCLAIMER

This book is designed to aid English-Spanish court interpreters by providing terms and related vocabulary used in U.S. court settings by criminalists, testifying as expert witnesses. It is sold with the understanding that the publisher and author are not engaged in rendering legal services and advice. If legal or other expert assistance is required, the services of a competent professional should be sought.

This compilation of forensic terminology is by no means all-inclusive, nor is it intended as a substitute for specialized dictionaries. There are certainly alternative ways to interpret or translate any given forensic term. There may be mistakes, both typographical and in content. The author and publisher shall have neither liability nor responsibility to any person or entity with respect to any loss or damage caused, or alleged to be caused, directly or indirectly by the information contained in this book.

ACKNOWLEDGEMENTS

I would like to thank the San Francisco Police Department, the International Association of Identification, and Infobase Publishing for their assistance with relevant material, as well as Dede Tisone, Georgette Baker, and Jason Kopp for their assistance with the cover and layout.

Ballistics

Balística

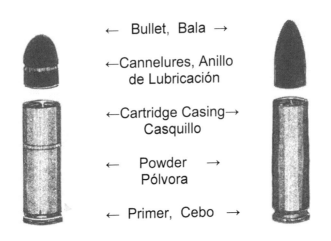

← Bullet, Bala →

←Cannelures, Anillo
de Lubricación

←Cartridge Casing→
Casquillo

← Powder →
Pólvora

← Primer, Cebo →

Handgun Cartridge

Rifle Cartridge

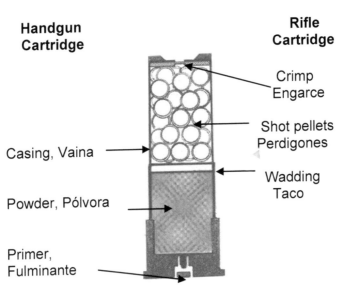

Casing, Vaina →

Powder, Pólvora →

Primer,
Fulminante →

Crimp
Engarce

Shot pellets
Perdigones

Wadding
Taco

Cutaway view of shotgun cartridge

Criminalistics for Spanish↔English Interpreters

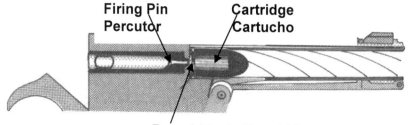

Firing Pin
Percutor

Cartridge
Cartucho

Breechblock, Espaldón

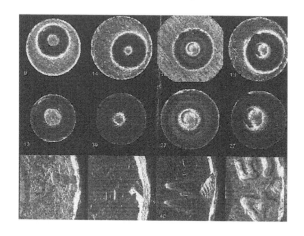

**Cartridge Case Markings caused
by the Breechblock, Firing Pin and Extractor**

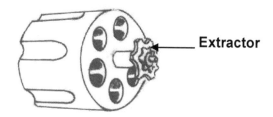

Extractor

Revolver Cylinder, Tambor de un Revólver

Ballistics

Balística

English	Español
abrasive paste	pasta esmeril
action	acción, mecanismo
alloy	aleación
angle of impact	ángulo de incidencia
antimony	antimonio
anvil	yunque
assault rifle	fusil automático
automatic pistol	pistola automática, escuadra
barium	bario
barrel	cañón
barrel twist	dirección del estriado
base wad	taco de base
blank	bala de fogueo, salva
bolt	cerrojo
bolt action	mecanismo de cerrojo
bore	ánima
brass (fired cartridge case)	casquillo, vaina
breech	recámara
breech loading	(de) retrocarga
breech marks	marcas de la recámara
breechblock marks	marcas del espaldón, marcas del bloque de cierre
bullet wipe	ahumamiento
bullet	proyectil, bala
butt	culata, cacha
caliber	calibre
cannelure ring	anillo de lubricación
cartridge	cartucho
cartridge casing	vainilla, vaina, casquillo, funda
casing	casquillo, funda, vaina
cast or stamped	estampado

Ballistics	Balística
center fire ammunition	municiones de percusión central
chamber	recámara
charcoal	carbón
checkering	estriado helicoidal
clip	peine
cock (v)	amartillar
cocking piece	palanca de armar
comparison	confrontación, cotejo
contact wound	herida a quemarropa, herida a bocajarro
contusion ring	bandeleta contusiva
crimp	doblez, engarce
crimp sealed	engarzado a presión
cylinder	tambor
deface	desfigurar, alterar
defacement	deformación, desfiguración
dent	abolladura
dent (v)	abollar
depth	profundidad
dermal nitrate test	prueba del guantelete
detonator cap	cápsula fulminante
diphenylamine sulfonate	sulfato de difenilamina
dud	cartucho o bala que no estalla
ejector	expulsor, botador
embed	incrustar
entry wound	orificio de entrada
etching agent	reactivo químico
exit wound	orificio de salida
extractor marks	marcas del extractor
file (v)	limar
filed off	lijado

Ballistics	Balística
firearms comparison	cotejo de armas de fuego
firing pin	percutor, aguja percutora
firing pin indentations	hendiduras de percutor
flammable	inflamable
flash suppressor	apagallamas
flight pattern	movimiento del proyectil, desplazamiento
fluting	estriado, rayado
force of impact	fuerza de impacto
fore grip	empuñadura delantera
front loading	de avancarga
front site	punto de mira
gauge (n)	calibre de escopeta
gouge (n)	boquete
grinding	pulido
grip	empuñadura
grip safety	seguro de la empuñadura
grooved bore	ánima rayada
grooves	estrías, rayas
GSR- gunshot residue	residuos del fulminato o de pólvora combustionada
hammer	percutor, martillo
handgun	arma corta
helical grooves	estriado helicoidal
hit the target	incidir en el blanco
hollow point	de punta hueca
holster	funda, pistolera
jacket	camisa, coraza
jacketed	encamisado, blindado
lands	campos
lead	plomo

Ballistics	Balística
left-handed	zurdo
lever	palanca
lubrication ring	anillo de lubricación
machine gun	ametralladora
magazine	cargador
magazine base	base del cargador
make	marca
manufacturer	fabricante
mar	dañar, estropear
misfire	tirar en falso, fallar
model	modelo
muzzle	boca
neutron activation analysis	análisis por activación de neutrones
nick, chip (v)	mellar
nitrate products	productos nitrados
nitric acid	ácido nítrico
nitrocellulose	nitrocelulosa
nose	ojiva, punta
nose configuration	perfil de la punta
obliterate	erradicar, borrar
obliteration of serial number	erradicación del número de serie
over-stamp	regrabar
over-stamping	regrabado
paraffin	parafina
paraffin gauntlet test	prueba del guantelete
paraffin mold	molde de parafina
path	trayectoria, recorrido
percussion cap	cápsula fulminante
pistol	pistola
pistol grip	puño de pistola, empuñadura

Ballistics	Balística
potassium nitrate	nitrato de potasio
powder tattooing	tatuaje
primer	cebo, fulminante
propellant	propulsante
pump action	de mecanismo de corredera
questioned bullet	proyectil problema
range	alcance
reagent	reactivo
recoil	retroceso
retail gun dealer	corredor de armas
reveal (v)	revenir
revolver	revolver
ricochet	rebote
rifle	fusil, rifle
rifled bore	ánima rayada, ánima estriada
rifling	rayado, estriado
right-handed	diestro
rim	reborde
	municiones de percusión
rimfire ammunition	periférica
round	balazo, tiro
	de cabo redondeado,
round-nose	de punta ojival
safety lever	llave de seguridad
sawed-off shotgun	escopeta recortada
scatter shot	perdigones
scope rings	anillos del visor
scorching	quemadura
scratch	ralladura
sear	fiador
semi-jacketed	semi encamisado
serial number	número de serie

Ballistics	Balística
serial number restoration	regeneración de marcas seriales
shards of metal	esquirlas de metal
shotgun	escopeta
shoulder weapon	arma de cañón largo
side-by-side	yuxtapuesto
sides	costados
silencer	silenciador
slide	corredera
slug	balín
smokeless powder	pólvora sin humo
smooth bore	ánima lisa
smudge ring	ahumamiento
sniper	francotirador
snub nose	de cañón chato
soft-point	de punta blanda
spectrometer	espectrómetro, espectroscopio
spent cartridge casing	casquillo (gastado)
stippling	tatuaje
striation	estría
striking energy	fuerza de impacto
sulphur	azufre
tattooing	tatuaje
Teflon coated bullets	balas revestidas de Teflón
test bullet	bala patrón
test firing	disparo experimental
title history	documentación de titularidad
trajectory rod	sedal, sonda acanalada
trigger	gatillo, disparador
trigger guard	guardamonte
trigger handle	asa del gatillo

Ballistics

unburned particles
wadding
water tank or trap
yaw
zip gun

Balística

granulaciones incombustas
taco
tanque de tiro
ladear
arma de fuego casero

Land **Groove**

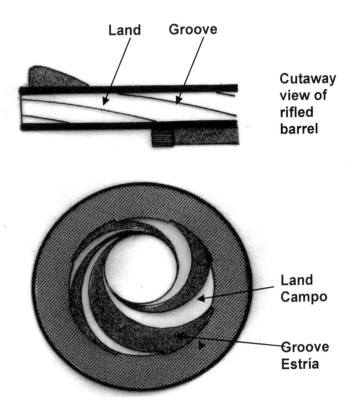

Cutaway
view of
rifled
barrel

Land
Campo

Groove
Estría

**View into the barrel of a firearm
with a righthand twist**

Ballistics   Balística

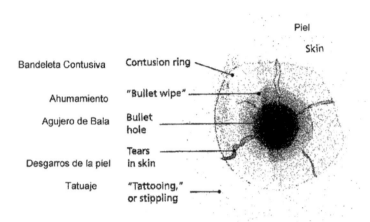

Piel

Skin

Bandeleta Contusiva	Contusion ring
Ahumamiento	"Bullet wipe"
Agujero de Bala	Bullet hole
Desgarros de la piel	Tears in skin
Tatuaje	"Tattooing," or stippling

General Characteristics of a Bullet Wound
(re-printed with the permission of Infobase Publlishing)

Striations
Estrías

Markings left on bullet by lands and grooves

Cause of Death	Causa de la Muerte
accidental death	muerte accidental
arteriosclerosis	arteriosclerosis
asphyxia	asfixia
beaten to death	matada a golpes
bleed out	desangramiento, desangrar
blunt force trauma	trauma ocasionado por fuerza contundente, golpe contuso
broken neck	desnucamiento
burns	quemaduras
carbon monoxide poisoning	envenenamiento por monóxido de carbono
cardiac arrest	paro cardíaco, fallo cardíaco
dismembered	desmembración
drowning	ahogamiento
drug overdose	sobredosis de drogas
electrocution	electrocución
exsanguination	desangramiento
gunshot wound	herida de bala
hanging	ahorcamiento
heart attack	infarto, ataque al corazón
homicide	homicidio
internal hemorrhaging	hemorragia interna
intoxication	intoxicación
manslaughter	homicidio sin premeditación
mortal wound	lesión o herida mortal
murder	homicidio
overdose	sobredosis
poisoning	envenenamiento
pulmonary edema	edema pulmonar
self-inflicted wound	lesión auto-infringida
sharp weapon	arma punzante

Cause of Death	Causa de la Muerte
slit throat	degollación
stab wound	herida de arma blanca, herida de puñalada
stabbing	apuñalamiento, apuñalada
strangulation	estrangulación
stroke	derrame cerebral
subdural hemorrhage	hematoma subdural
suffocation	asfixia
suicide	suicidio
traumatic shock	shock traumático

Chain of Custody	Cadena de Custodia
case number	número del caso
date	fecha
disposition	disposición, colocación
distinctive marks	marcas distintivas
evidence locker	depósito de pruebas
file number	número de expediente
handling	manipulación
heat-seal	cerrar herméticamente
label (n)	etiqueta, marbete
label (v)	etiquetar
log book	cuaderno de bitácora
official letter	oficio
origin	procedencia
package (v)	embalar, empaquetar,envasar
packaging	embalaje
place	lugar, ubicación
probative elements	elementos probatorios
reliable	fehaciente
resealable	que se puede volver a cerrar
safeguard	resguardar
seal	sellar
seal with wax	lacrar
shield number	número de insignia
special handling	manipulación segura
temperature	temperatura
time	hora

Explosives/Arson	Explosivos/Incendio Doloso
accelerant	acelerante
acetone	acetona
ANFO- ammonium nitrate fuel oil	cloratos y nitrato de amonio
ashes	cenizas
blast	onda explosiva
bomb disposal unit	comando anti-bomba
bomb remains	restos de explosivo
butane gas	gas butano
carbon monoxide	monóxido de carbono
casting	moldeo
creosote build-up	acumulación de creosota
delayed fuse	espoleta de retardo
detonator	detonador
flame	llama
flares	bengala
half burned	semicalcinado
high explosive	detonante
hoax bomb device	bomba falsa
homemade bomb	explosivo casero
IED - improvised explosive device	aparato o artefacto explosivo improvisado
igniter	encendedor
incendiary device	aparato incendiario
lacquer	laca
letter bomb	carta bomba
live explosive	explosivo activo
low explosive	deflagrante
methanol	metanol
Molotov cocktail	cóctel Molotov
paint thinner	disolvente de pintura

Explosives/Arson

petroleum distillates
pipe bomb
point of origin
propane
safety helmet
shock wave injury
shrapnel
soot
spark
switch
timing mechanism
turpentine
vaporize
water soluble

Explosivos/Incendio Doloso

solventes de hidrocarburos
bomba de tubo
foco del incendio
propano
casco
lesión por onda expansiva
metralla
hollín
chispa
interruptor
temporizador
trementina
pulverizar
soluble en agua

Criminalistics for Spanish↔English Interpreters

Fingerprints	Huellas Dactilares
accidental whorl	verticilo accidental
amino acid	aminoácido
arch	arco
arch pattern	dibujo de arcos
baby finger	meñique
bifurcation	bifurcación
body oil	depósito grasoso sudoríparo
brush	pincel
brushstroke	pincelada
bumpy, pitted	rugoso
central pocket loop whorls	lazos o verticilos de bolsa central
clean print	impresión nítida
constant	perenne
cyanoacrylate (super glue)	cianoacrilato (súper pegamento)
data storage system	sistema de almacenamiento de datos
delta	delta
dermis	dermis
development of fingerprints	revelado de huellas dactilares
digitally encode	cifrar digitalmente, encriptar
divergence	desviación
double loop whorls	lazos (o verticilos) gemelos
dragon's blood	sangre de drago
dust (v)	revelar
eccrine glands	glándulas sudoríparas
electrostatic copy toner	toner electrostático
enclosure	ojal
ends of ridges	puntos de crestas papilares
epidermis	epidermis
eyelet	ojal

Fingerprints	Huellas Dactilares
fingerprint	huella dactilar o digital, impresión dactilar
fingerprint card	ficha dactilar, dactilograma
fingerprint comparison	cotejo dactilar
fingerprint expert	perito en dactiloscopia
fingerprint pattern	dibujo de huellas dactilares
fingerprint powders	reveladores de huellas
fingerprint processor	procesadora de huellas
friction ridges	crestas papilares
fuming cabinet	cámara de vaporización, cámara de gases
furrows	surcos
Henry System	Sistema Henry
high speed reader	lectora de alta velocidad
in relief	en relieve
index finger	dedo índice
ink roller	rodillo
inked fingerprint card	dactilograma
iodine	yodo
known print	huella indubitada, huella modelo
laser illumination of prints	láser revelador de huellas
latent fingerprint	huella dactilar latente
loop	presilla, lazo
loop pattern	dibujo de presillas
magnetic fingerprint powder	polvo magnético
middle finger	dedo medio o cordial
ninhydrin	ninhidrina
non-porous	no poroso
oblique lighting	luz oblicua, luz reflejada
palm print	huella palmar
papillary ridges	crestas papilares

Fingerprints	Huellas Dactilares
plain arch	arco plano
plain whorl	torbellino
plaster of paris	yeso, escayola
plasticine	plastilina
points of identification	puntos característicos, minucias
pore	poro
powder	polvo
radial loop	presilla interna o radial
ridge island	ojal
ridge dot	punto
ridges	crestas
ring finger	dedo anular
screen wire	tela metálica
search and compare	búsqueda y confronte
sebaceous glands	glándulas sebáceas
silicone rubber putty	masilla de silicona
silver nitrate	nitrato de plata
sole of the foot	planta del pie
spray	pulverizar
sweat glands	glándulas sudoríparas
ten finger print	(impresión) decadactilar
tented arch	arco tendido
thumb	pulgar
tip of finger	punta, yema del dedo
ulnar loop	presilla externa o lunar, presilla cubital
unchangeable	inmutable
unknown print	huella dubitada
Vucetich System	Sistema Vucetich
whorl	verticilo
whorl pattern	dibujo de verticilo

Fingerprints

Fingerprint Patterns

Dibujos de Huellas

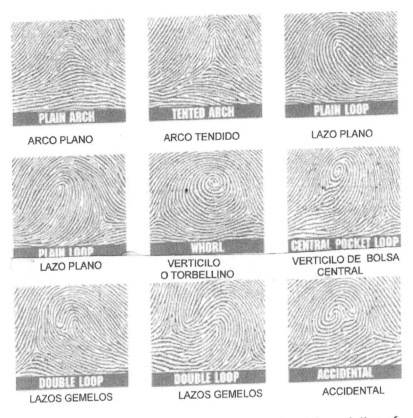

PLAIN ARCH	TENTED ARCH	PLAIN LOOP
ARCO PLANO	ARCO TENDIDO	LAZO PLANO
PLAIN LOOP	WHORL	CENTRAL POCKET LOOP
LAZO PLANO	VERTICILO O TORBELLINO	VERTICILO DE BOLSA CENTRAL
DOUBLE LOOP	DOUBLE LOOP	ACCIDENTAL
LAZOS GEMELOS	LAZOS GEMELOS	ACCIDENTAL

Fingerprint patterns (Courtesy of the International Association of Identification, IAI)

Questioned Documents	Documentos Dubitados
addition	añadido, agregado
binder	encolado
bleaching agent	decolorante
charred	calcinado, quemado
chromatography	cromatografía
class characteristic	propiedad grupo-específico
cursive writing	letra cursiva, letra de mano
damaged document	documento adulterado
digital imaging	editor de gráficos
enhancement	rasterizados
disguised handwriting	letra tergiversada, escrito disfrazado
dot matrix printer	impresora matriz de puntos
electrostatic detection apparatus	aparato de detección electrostático
embossing	en relieve
erasures	borrados
exemplar	ejemplar
facsimile signature	firma facsímil
falsify	falsificar
font	fuente
forge	adulterar, falsificar
forged document	documento falsificado
forgery	falsificación
high resolution scanner	escáner de alta definición
imperceptible	Impalpable
indentation	hendidura
indented writing	marcas en papel por apoyo al escribir
individual characteristics	elementos identificadores
inkjet printer	impresora inyección de tinta
iodine fuming	vapores de yodo

Questioned Documents	Documentos Dubitados
	documento de referencia,
known document	documento indubitado
laser printer	impresora láser
macroscopy	macroscopía
microscopy	microscopía
nib track	surcos dejados por bolígrafo
obliteration	eliminación, erradicación
patch	retocar
pen pressure	fuerza de apoyo
photocopy machine	(máquina) fotocopiadora
poison pen letters	anónimo ponzoñoso
questioned document	documento dubitado
ransom note	nota exigiendo un rescate
resin	resina
ribbon	cinta de tela
security thread	hilo de seguridad
slant	inclinación (de la escritura)
soak	macerar
spacing	espaciado
spectroscopy	espectroscopía
stampings	estampillados
stereomicroscope	estéreomicroscopio
thin-layer chromatography	cromatografía de capa fina
toner	toner
torn	roto
tracing	calcado
typed letter	carta mecanografiada
watermark	marca de agua
wood pulp	pulpa de madera

Rape/Sexual Assault	Violación/Agresión Sexual
acid phosphatase	fosfatasa ácida
agglutinin	aglutinina
air-dried	secado al aire
anal penetration	penetración anorrectal
anal speculum	espéculo anal
anus	ano
aspermia	aspermia
bite marks	marcas de dientes, mordeduras
breasts	mamas, senos
burn	quemadura
colposcope	colposcopio
control sample	muestra testigo, muestra control
contusion	contusión, moretón
crystal test	reacción microcristalográfica
date rape drug	droga de la violación
deviant behavior	conducta desviada o anormal
ecchymosis (bruise)	equimosis (moretón)
false positive	falso positivo
fingernail scrapings	residuos debajo de las uñas; mugre de las uñas
fluoresce	fluorescer
gag (n)	mordaza
genital area	zona genital
genital injuries using the face of a clock	desgarros genitales según el cuadrante horario
gynecological exam	examen ginecólogo
hematoma	hematoma
hold down	sujetar
hymeneal quadrant	cuadrante himeneal
laceration	laceración

Rape/Sexual Assault	Violación/Agresión Sexual
mouth lesion	lesión bucal
needle mark	puntura de inyección, pinchazo
non-consensual	sin consentimiento
perineum	periné
physical exam	examen físico
presumptive test	prueba de orientación
psychiatric exam	estudio psiquiátrico
pubic area	zona púbica
pubic hair	pelo del pubis
sadistic	sádico
seminal acid phosphatase	fosfatasa ácida en el semen
sex offender	delincuente sexual
sharp point	borde filoso o cortante
signs of violence	rastros de violencia
smear	frotis
sodomy	sodomía
speculum	espéculo
sperm	esperma
spermatozoa	espermatozoide
superficial cut	lesión incisa superficial
tearing	desgarros
tearing of the perineum	desgarros perineales
tie down	atar
traces of strangulation with a rope	signos de estrangulamiento con lazo
ultra-violet light	luz ultravioleta
vagina	vagina
vaginal cavity	cavidad vaginal
vaginal penetration	penetración vaginal
vaginal smear slide	frotis vaginal

Rape/Sexual Assault

vaginal walls
vulva region
wooden splint
Wood's lamp

Violación/Agresión Sexual

paredes vaginales
zona vulvar
tablilla
aparato de luz de Wood

Forensic Serology	Serología Forense
ABO typing	sistema ABO
allele	alelo
antibodies	anticuerpos
antigen	antígeno
arterial gushing	brote arterial
benzidine	bencidina
biochemistry	bioquímica
blood analysis	análisis de sangre
blood clots	coágulos
blood sample	muestra de sangre
blood spatter analysis	análisis de salpicaduras de sangre
blood stream	reguero de sangre
blood trace	rastros sanguinolentos
blood trail	reguero de sangre
blood type	grupo sanguíneo
bloodstain	mancha de sangre
bloodstain pattern	manchas de sangre, patrón de la mancha de sangre
breached artery	arteria seccionada
bubble rings	anillos de burbujas
cast-off pattern	manchas por proyección
clots	coágulos
collect	recolectar
control sample	muestra de control
directionality	dirección de la proyección
directionality angle	ángulo de dirección
dried blood	sangre desecada
dropper	gotero
drops	gotas
false positive	falso positivo
forensic hematology	hematología forense

Forensic Serology	Serología Forense
hemin crystals	cristales de clorhidrato de hematina
hemoglobin	hemoglobina
hemorrhage	hemorragia
high velocity pattern	proyección a gran velocidad
hydrogen peroxide	peróxido de hidrógeno
impact angle	ángulo de incidencia
infrared light	rayos infrarrojos
Kastle-Meyer color test	reacción Kastle-Meyer
kinship	consanguinidad
luminol	luminol
momentum	velocidad, momento
morphology	morfología
nosebleed	hemorragia nasal
phenolphthalein	fenolftaleina
pool of blood	laguna o charco de sangre
presumptive test	prueba de orientación
red blood cells	glóbulos rojos
RH factor	factor RH
soak	impregnar
sodium carbonate	carbonato sódico
spatter	salpicaduras
spot	mácula, mancha
stained	maculado, manchado
sterile saline solution	solución salina estéril
surface	superficie, soporte
tadpole shape	en forma de renacuajo
traces of blood	rastros sanguinolentos
velocity impact	velocidad de la proyección

Forensic Serology   Serología Forense

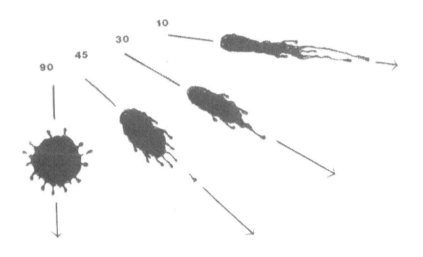

Bloodstain patterns by angle of impact

Criminalistics for Spanish↔English Interpreters

Tools of the Trade	Herramientas del Oficio
acid	ácido
blotting paper	papel secante
bottle	botella, frasco
brush	pincel
Bunsen burner	mechero Bunsen
carbon paper	papel carbón
cellophane	papel celofán
clay	arcilla
clipboard	tablilla con sujetapapeles
colored chalk	tizas de colores
comparison microscope	microscopio de comparación
compass	brújula, compás
coverall	overol, mono
darkroom	cuarto oscuro
decameter	decámetro
diphenylamine	difenilamina
disposable gloves	guantes desechables
distilled water	agua destilada
dust pan	recogedor
emission spectrograph	analizador de espectro óptico
envelopes	sobres
ethyl alcohol	alcohol etílico
eye dropper	gotero
face shield	visor facial, protector facial
filter paper	papel filtro
flashlight	linterna
flask	matraz
fluoroscope	fluoroscopio
forceps	fórceps, tenazas, pinzas
fuming cabinet	cámara de vaporización,
gas chromatography	cromatografía de gases

Tools of the Trade

Herramientas del Oficio

goggles	gafas protectoras
graph paper	papel cuadriculado
hard hat	casco
high performance liquid chromatography (HPLC)	cromatografía líquida de alto rendimiento
high-speed reader	lectora de alta velocidad
ink roller	rodillo
inkpad	placa para la tinta, tampón
jar	frasco, envase
lab coat	bata blanca
lab kit	maletín o estuche de trabajo
label	etiqueta
lie detector	detector de mentiras
lime	cal
litmus paper	papel tornasol
luminol	luminol
magnifying glass	lupa
mass spectrometer	espectrómetro de masas
measuring tape	cinta métrica
microscope	microscopio
microspectrometer	microespectroscopio
microspectrophotometer	microespectroscopio
mixing bowl	bol o tazón
notebook	cuaderno, libreta
paper box	caja de cartón
pedometer	podómetro
penknife	cortaplumas
petri dish	plato de laboratorio
phenolphthalein	fenolfateína
photomicrography	fotomicrografía
pipette	pipeta

Tools of the Trade	Herramientas del Oficio
plaster	escayola, yeso
plastic bag	bolsa de plástico
plumb line	plomada
polygraph	detector de mentiras
print processor	procesadora de huellas
Q tips	hisopos, bastoncillo de algodón
rubber gloves	guantes de hule
ruler	regla
safety helmet	casco protector
saline solution	solución salina
scalpel	bisturí
sealing wax	lacre
shoe covers	cubre zapatos
slide	portaobjetos
sound spectrograph	espectrógrafo acústico
spectrometer	espectrómetro
spectrophotometer	espectrofotómetro
spectroscope	espectroscopio
splint	tablilla
spray bottle	pulverizador
stearic acid	ácido esteárico
stereomicroscope	estéreomicroscopio
sterilizing equipment	equipo esterilizador
stool	taburete
stopper	tapa, tapón
surgical cap	gorro quirúrgico
syringe	jeringa
tape	cinta adhesiva
tape recorder	grabadora
test tube	tubo de ensayo

Tools of the Trade

Herramientas del Oficio

thin layer chromatography	cromatografía de capa fina
tongue depressor	aplicador de madera
tripod	trípode
vial	ampolla, frasco
video camera	cámara de video
white cloth	tela blanca
Wood's lamp	aparato de luz de Wood
X ray diffraction unit	difractor de rayos X

Trace	Rastros
accidental characteristic	rastro único, elemento identificador
bite marks	marcas de dientes, mordeduras
bleach	cloro, lejía
brush	pincel
burn marks	signos de quemadura
cast (n)	moldeado, molde, vaciado
cast (v)	vaciar
cellophane	celofán
chip	astilla
citrate	citrato
class characteristic	propiedad grupo específico
cleated sole	suela claveteada
cloth fiber	fibra textil
clothes fiber	rastro vestimenta, rastro indumentario
cord	cordel, cuerda
crowbar	palanca
defacement	alteración, deformación
dent (n)	abolladura
displace	desplazar
dump (v)	tirar, botar
dye	tinta
enhance	aumentar, ampliar
fiber	fibra
filing	lijado, limado
fingernail scrapings	mugre de las uñas, residuos debajo de las uñas
finish (n)	acabado
flaking (of the skin)	piel descamada
flat surface	plano o soporte liso

Trace	Rastros
fleck	partícula, mota
footprint	huella de pisada descalza
footprint (human)	huella de pisada (humana)
glass container	recipiente de vidrio
glass fragment	trozo de cristal, trozo de vidrio
gouge (v)	abrir, hacer una ranura
gravel	grava
grinding	pulido
grouping	acopio
hair	cabello, pelo
hair spray	laca, fijador
imbedded	incrustado
individual characteristic	característica singular, elemento identificador
IR light	luz infrarroja
jagged	irregular
layer	capa
manufacturer	fabricante
metallic dust	polvo metálico, limadura
mold (n)	moldeado, molde, vaciado
nick	muesca
obliterate	erradicar
origin	procedencia
over-stamp (v)	regrabar
packaging	embalaje
paint chip	astilla de pintura, raspado de pintura
palm	palma de la mano
partial print	huella fragmentaria
particle	partícula
paw print	huella de pisada animal
pinpoint	establecer con exactitud

Trace	Rastros
plaster	escayola, yeso
powder	talco
preserve	conservar, preservar
print	huella, reseña
processing of trace evidence	procesamiento de rastros
pry marks	marcas de palanca
pull out	arrancar
reference sample	muestra de referencia
relief	relieve
remains	residuos, restos
rip	rasgar, romper
rubber sole	suela de caucho
rule out	descartar
safe insulation	aisladoras de cajas fuertes
saw (n)	sierra, serrucho
sawdust	serrín
scale reference	referencia de escala
scrape (v)	raspar
scratch (n)	arañazo, ralladura
screen wire	tela metálica
search (n)	registro
semen	semen
shard	fragmento
shaving	viruta
shellac	laca
shoe print	huella de pisada calzada
sift (v)	tamizar
signs of struggle	señales de forcejeo
smear with	embadurnar de
sole of shoe	suela del zapato

Trace	Rastros
spray (v)	pulverizar, rociar
spray paint (v)	pintar con atomizador
stain	mancha
stopper	tapa
string	cordel, hilo
sweat	sudor, transpiración
symptom	síntoma
tape	cinta adhesiva
tape lift (v)	levantar con cinta adhesiva
tarnished	deslustrado
teeth marks	huellas de dientes
thread	hilo
timeline	cronología
tire marks	huellas de neumáticos, marcas de llantas
tool marks	marcas o huellas de herramientas
tooth marks	huellas de dientes
torn	roto, rasgado
trace elements	elementos trazadores
tracking dog	perro rastreador
UV light	luz ultravioleta
vacuum packed	envasado al vacío
vat	tanque, cuba
water mark	marcas de agua
wax paper	papel parafinado
wear pattern	patrón de desgaste, de uso
wood sliver	astilla
worn area	zona desgastada

Weapons	Armas
arrow	flecha
automatic rifle	fusil automático
ax	hacha
BB gun	carabina de aire comprimido
billy club	porra
blunt weapon	arma contundente
bolt cutter	cortapernos
box cutter	cortador de cajas
brass knuckles	nudilleras, manoplas
cobblestone	adoquín
commando knife	cuchillo de combate
crossbow	ballesta
crowbar	palanca
cutting instrument	instrumento cortante
dagger	puñal, daga
double-edged sword	espada de dos filos
file	lima
firearm	arma de fuego
hacksaw	sierra de arco
hammer	martillo
ice pick	punzón
jackknife	navaja
knife	cuchillo
machete	machete
machine gun	ametralladora
nail	clavo
nightstick	porra
nunchuks	chacos
paving stone	adoquín
pellet gun	carabina de posta
piercing instrument	instrumento perforante

Weapons

Weapons	Armas
pin	alfiler
pistol	pistola
razor blade	hojilla (hoja) de afeitar
revolver	revólver
rifle	fusil, rifle
screwdriver	destornillador
semi-automatic rifle	fusil semiautomático
sharp instrument	instrumento punzante
sickle	hoz (f)
sledgehammer	almádena
steel pipe	tubo de acero
stick	palo
straight razor	navaja barbera
	navaja de mil usos,
Swiss army knife	navaja múltiple
switchblade	navaja de resorte
sword	espada
table knife	cuchillo de mesa
walking stick	bastón

Criminalistics	Criminalística
ABO typing	sistema ABO
abrasion	excoriación
abrasive	abrasivo
abrasive paste	pasta esmeril
accelerant	acelerante
accessory after the fact	encubridor
accidental characteristic	rastro único, elemento identificador
accidental death	muerte accidental
accidental whorl	verticilo accidental
accomplice	cómplice
acetone	acetona
acid	ácido
acid phosphatase	fosfatasa ácida
action	acción, mecanismo
acute contusion	contusión aguda
acute hemorrhage	hemorragia aguda
addition	añadido, agregado
adhesive base	base de adhesión
advanced stage of decomposition	en avanzado estado de descomposición
affix	fijar
agglutinin	aglutinina
air-dried	secado al aire
allele	alelo
alloy	aleación
amino acid	aminoácido
anal penetration	penetración anorrectal
anal speculum	espéculo anal
analyze	analizar
anatomical exam	examen anatómico

Criminalistics	Criminalística
ANFO-ammonium nitrate fuel oil	cloratos y nitrato de amonio
angle of impact	ángulo de incidencia
animal hair	pelo animal
animal prints	huellas de pisadas animales
annotate	acotar
anterior surface	superficie o cara anterior
anthropometrics	antropometría
antibodies	anticuerpos
antigen	antígeno
antimony	antimonio
anus	ano
anvil	yunque
arch	arco
arch pattern	dibujo de arcos
arches	arcos
arrive at a reliable result	obtener un resultado fidedigno
arrow	flecha
arsenic	arsénico
arson	incendio doloso
arterial spurting	brote arterial
arteriosclerosis	arteriosclerosis
ashes	cenizas
aspermia	aspermia
asphyxia	asfixia
assault rifle	fusil automático
automatic pistol	pistola automática, escuadra
automatic rifle	fusil automático
autopsy	autopsia
awkward situation	situación engorrosa
ax	hacha

Criminalistics	Criminalística
baby finger	meñique
backlog	atraso
backup record	registro de reserva
ballistics	balística
ballistics expert	perito en balística
banister	baranda, barandilla
bar chart	gráfico de barras
bare (bone)	descarnado (hueso)
barefoot print	huella de pisada descalza
barium	bario
barrel (of a gun)	cañón (de un arma de fuego)
barrel twist	dirección del estriado
base wad	taco de base
BB gun	carabina de aire comprimido
beaker	vaso de precipitados
beat up (v)	propinar una paliza o golpiza
beaten to death	matada a golpes
beating	golpiza, paliza
benzidine	bencidina
bifurcation	bifurcación
billy club	porra
bind	enlazar
binder	encolado
biochemistry	bioquímica
biohazard	peligro biológico
bite marks	marcas de dientes, mordedura
blank	bala de fogueo, salva
blast	onda explosiva
bleach	cloro, lejía
bleaching agent	decolorante
bleed out	desangrar, morir desangrado

Criminalistics	Criminalística
bleeding	hemorragia
blood analysis	análisis de sangre
blood clot	coágulo
blood drop	gota de sangre
blood sample	muestra de sangre
blood spatter	salpicadura de sangre
blood spatter analysis	análisis de salpicadura de sangre
blood stream	reguero de sangre
blood trace	rastros sanguinolentos
blood trail	reguero de sangre
blood type	grupo sanguíneo
bloodstain	mancha de sangre
bloodstain patterns	manchas de sangre
bloodstained	ensangrentado
blotting paper	papel secante
bludgeon	aporrear
blunt force trauma	trauma ocasionado por fuerza contundente, golpe contuso
blunt weapon	arma contundente
bodily fluids	fluidos corporales
body oil	depósito grasoso sudoríparo
bolt	cerrojo
bolt action	mecanismo de cerrojo
bolt cutter	cortapernos
bomb attack	atentado con bomba
bomb disposal unit	comando anti-bomba
bomb remains	restos de explosivo
bone fragment	esquirla ósea
bore (of a gun)	ánima
bottle	botella, frasco
bottle (v)	envasar

Criminalistics	Criminalística
box cutter	cortador de cajas
brass (fired cartridge case)	casquillo, vaina
brass knuckles	nudilleras, manoplas
breached artery	arteria seccionada
breakage	rotura
breast implant	implante de seno
breasts	mamas, senos
breech	recámara
breech loading	(de) retrocarga
breech marks	marcas de la recámara
breechblock marks	marcas del espaldón, marcas del bloque de cierre
bristly	hirsuto
broadly	en grandes líneas
broken neck	desnucamiento
bruising	contusiones, morretones
brush	pincel
brushstroke	pincelada
brutal attack	ataque salvaje
bubble rings	anillos de burbujas
buffer solution	solución buffer
bullet	proyectil, bala
bullet hole	agujero de bala
bullet jacket	envoltura (de bala)
bullet to the head	balazo en la cabeza
bullet wipe	ahumamiento
bumpy	rugoso
Bunsen burner	mechero Bunsen
burn (n)	quemadura
burn marks	signos de quemadura

Criminalistics	Criminalística
	el cuerpo presenta calcinado
burns over 80 % of the	en un 80% de la superficie
body	corporal
butane gas	gas butano
butt (of a firearm)	culata, cacha
buttock implant	implante en las nalgas
bystander	espectador
cadaver	cadáver
caliber	calibre
callus	callos
cannelure ring	anillo de lubricación
carbon monoxide	monóxido de carbono
carbon monoxide	envenenamiento por monóxido
poisoning	de carbono
carbon paper	papel carbón
card of contrasting colors	tarjeta de colores opuestos
cardboard box	caja de cartón
cardiac arrest	paro cardíaco, fallo cardíaco
careful search	registro minucioso
cartridge	cartucho
cartridge casings	vainilla, vaina, casquillo
case number	número del caso
casing	casquillo, funda, vaina
cast (n)	moldeado, molde, vaciado
cast (v)	vaciar
casting	moldeo
cast-off pattern	manchas por proyección
catalyst	catalizador
caulk	calafateo, enmasillado
cavity	fosa
cellophane	papel celofán
cellophane envelope	sobre de celofán

Criminalistics	Criminalística
center fire ammunition	municiones de percusión central
central pocket loop whorls	verticilos de bolsa central
chain of custody	cadena de custodia
chain saw	motosierra
chamber	recámara
chances	posibilidad, probabilidad
charcoal	carbón
charred	calcinado, quemado
chart	gráfico
checkering	estriado helicoidal
chemical process	procedimiento químico
chip	astilla, raspado
chromatography	cromatografía
cigarette butt	colilla de cigarrillo
citrate	citrato
class characteristic	propiedad grupo-específico
clay	arcilla
clean print	impresión nítida
clear the area	despejar el lugar
cleated sole	suela claveteada
clip	peine, cargador
clipboard	tablilla con sujetapapeles
close-up	vista en detalle, foto en primer plano
cloth fiber	fibra textil
clothes fiber	rastro vestimenta
clothes fragment	trozo de ropa
clothing fiber	fibra de tela
clots	coágulos
clotted blood	sangre coagulada
clue	clave, pista

Criminalistics	Criminalística
cobblestone	adoquín
cock (v)	amartillar
cocking piece	palanca de armar
collect	recolectar
collect data	recabar datos
collect, preserve, evaluate	obtener, preservar y valorar
collection of evidence	recopilación de pruebas
color film	película pancromática
colored chalk	tizas de colores
colposcope	colposcopio
commando knife	cuchillo de combate
comparison	confrontación, cotejo
comparison microscope	microscopio de comparación
compass	brújula, compás
composite sketch	retrato compuesto
computer enhancement	técnicas de informática forense
concealment	ocultamiento
conclusively	de manera concluyente
congenital	congénito
consistent with	consecuente, congruente con
constant	perenne
contact wound	herida a quemarropa, a bocajarro
container	envase, recipiente
contaminant	contaminante
contaminate	contaminar
contour	contorno
control sample	elemento "testigo"; muestra de control
contusion ring	bandeleta contusiva
contusion	contusión, moretón
cord	cordel

Criminalistics	Criminalística
cordon off	acordonar, cercar con sogas
counterfeit (n)	falsificación
cover letter	oficio
coverall	overol, mono
crawl space	espacio vacío, pasadizo, cavidad
creosote build-up	acumulación de creosota
crescent wrench	llave de boca
crevice	grieta
criminalist	criminalista, científico forense
criminalistics	criminalística
crimp	doblez, engarce, estrechadura
crimp sealed	engarzado a presión
cross section	corte transversal
crossbow	ballesta
crossfire	cruce de balas
crowbar	palanca
cryptanalysis	criptografía
cryptography	criptografía
crystal test	reacción microcristalográfica
cuffs	puños
culture	cultivo
cursive writing	letra cursiva, letra de mano
cursory examination	examen superficial o somero
cut	cortada
cuticle	cutícula
cutting agent	adulterante
cutting instrument	instrumento cortante
cyanoacrylate (super glue)	cianoacrilato(súper pegamento)
cylinder	tambor
dagger	puñal, daga

Criminalistics	Criminalística
damaged document	documento adulterado
darkroom	cuarto oscuro
data base	base de datos
data storage system	sistema de almacenamiento de datos
date	fecha
date (v)	fechar
date rape drug	droga de la violación
death certificate	acta de defunción
debris	escombros, restos, desechos
decameter	decámetro
decapitate	decapitar
decay	descomposición
deceased	finado, fallecido
decomposition	descomposición
deface	desfigurar, alterar, enmascarar
defacement	deformación, alteración
defensive wounds	lesiones de defensa
degrade	degradar, deteriorar
delayed fuse	espoleta de retardo
deltas	deltas
dent	abolladura
dent (v)	abollar
dentures	dentadura postiza
depressions	depresiones
depth	profundidad
dermal nitrate test	prueba del guantelete
dermis	dermis
desiccated	seco
detachment	desprendimiento
detonator	detonador
detonator cap	cápsula fulminante

Criminalistics	Criminalística
develop (film)	revelar (película)
development of fingerprints	revelado de huellas dactilares
deviant behavior	conducta desviada o anormal
digital imaging enhancement	editor de gráficos rasterizados
digitally encode	cifrar digitalmente, encriptar
diphenylamine	difenilamina
diphenylamine sulfonate	sulfato de difenilamina
direct observation	observación directa
direction of travel	dirección de desplazamiento
directionality	dirección de proyección
directionality angle	ángulo de proyección
disappear, fade	desvanecer
disguised handwriting	letra tergiversada, escrito disfrazado
disinterment	exhumación
dismember	desmembrar
dismembered	desmembración
displace	desplazar
disposable gloves	guantes desechables
disposition	disposición, colocación
dissect	disecar
distilled water	agua destilada
distinctive marks	marcas distintivas
distinguishing marks	señas particulares
divergence	desviación
DNA - deoxyribonucleic acid	ADN -ácido desoxirribonucleico
DNA typing	tipificación del ADN
do not line up	no se alinean
dot matrix printer	impresora matriz de puntos

Criminalistics / Criminalística

Criminalistics	Criminalística
double-edged sword	espada de dos filos
double loop whorls	lazos (o verticilos) gemelos
dragon's blood	sangre de drago
draw a sketch	hacer un croquis
drawback	inconveniente, desventaja
drawing to scale	croquis a escala
dried blood	sangre desecada
dropper	gotero
drops	gotas
drowning	ahogamiento
drug overdose	sobredosis de drogas
dry out	desecar
duct tape	cinta industrial, cinta metálica
dud	cartucho o bala que no estalla
dumb evidence	testigo mudo
dump (v)	tirar, botar
dumping ground	vertedero
dust (v) (for prints)	revelar
dust pan	recogedor
dye	tinta
ecchymosis (bruise)	equimosis (moretón)
eccrine glands	glándulas sudoríparas
edema	edema
ejaculation	eyaculación
ejector	expulsor, botador
elapsed time	tiempo trascurrido
electrocution	electrocución
electrostatic copy toner	toner electrostático
electrostatic detection apparatus	aparato de detección electrostático
embalming fluid	líquido de embalsamar

Criminalistics	Criminalística
embed	incrustar
embossing	en relieve
emission spectrograph	analizador de espectro óptico, espectrógrafo
empirical	empírico
encephalic matter	material encefálico
enclosure (fingerprint pattern)	ojal
ends of ridges	puntos de crestas papilares
enhance	aumentar, ampliar
enlarged photograph	fotografía ampliada
entomologist	entomólogo
entry route	vía de acceso
entry wound	orificio de entrada
envelopes	sobres
epidermis	epidermis
epithelial cell	epitelio, célula epitelial
epithelium	epitelio, célula epitelial
erasures	borrados
escape route	vía de huida
etching agent	reactivo químico
ethyl alcohol	alcohol etílico
evaluate the evidence	valorar la prueba
evidence container	envase,recipiente para pruebas
evidence locker	depósito de pruebas
evidence of violence	trazas de violencia
exemplar	ejemplar
exhumation	exhumación
exit wound	orificio de salida
expert's report	dictamen pericial
exsanguination	desangramiento
extractor marks	marcas del extractor

Criminalistics	Criminalística
exude from	rezumar de
eye dropper	gotero
eyelet	ojal
eyewear	gafas protectoras
face down	boca abajo
face shield	visor facial, protector facial
face up	boca arriba
facial reconstruction	reconstrucción cráneo-facial
facsimile signature	firma facsímil
fade	desvanecer
faker	simulador
false positive	falso positivo
falsify	adulterar, falsificar
fastener	cierre, presilla, sujetador
fatal wound	herida de muerte
feathers	plumas
fetish	fetiche
fetishist	fetichista
fiber	fibra
field	descampado
field investigation	criminalística de campo
file (n)	lima
file (v)	limar
file number	número de expediente
file off	lijar
filed off	borrado por limado
filing	lijado
filling (of a tooth)	empaste, amalgama
filter paper	papel filtro
findings	hallazgos
fingerlike projections	salientes en forma de rayos

Criminalistics	Criminalística
	residuos debajo de las uñas,
fingernail scrapings	mugre de las uñas
fingerprint	huella digital, impresión dactilar
fingerprint card	ficha dactilar, dactilograma
fingerprint comparison	cotejo dactilar
fingerprint expert	perito en dactiloscopia
fingerprint pattern	dibujo de huellas dactilares
fingerprint powders	reveladores de huellas
fingerprint processor	procesadora de huellas
finish (n)	acabado
firearm	arma de fuego
firearms comparison	cotejo de armas de fuego
fireball	bola de fuego
firing pin	percutor, aguja percutora
firing pin indentations	hendiduras de percutor
first degree burns	quemaduras de primer grado
flake	hojuela
flaking (of the skin)	piel descamada
flame	llama
flammable	inflamable
flap	solapa
flare	bengala
flash suppressor	apaga llamas
flashlight	linterna
flask	matraz
flat surface	plano o suporte liso
flaw	desperfecto
fleck	mota, salpicadura, partícula
	movimiento del proyectil,
flight pattern	desplazamiento
flow (v)	correr
fluoresce	fluorescer

Criminalistics	Criminalística
fluoroscope	fluoroscopio
fluting	estría
follicle	folículo piloso
follicular tissue	tejido folicular
font	fuente
footprint (human)	huella de pisada (humana)
force of impact	fuerza de impacto
forced entry	entrada forzada
forceps	fórceps, tenazas, pinzas
fore grip	empuñadura delantera
forensic art	dibujo forense
forensic chemistry	química forense
forensic hematology	hematología forense
forensic science	criminalística, ciencia forense
forge	adulterar, falsificar
forged document	documento falsificado
foul play	circunstancia oscura
fracture	fractura
fragment of clothing	trozo de vestido
frequency	periodicidad
friction ridges	crestas papilares
front loading	de avancarga
front site	punto de mira
fumes	gases
fuming cabinet	cámara de vaporización, cámara de gases
furrows	surcos
fuse (n)	espoleta
gag (n)	mordaza
gas chromatography	cromatografía de gases

Criminalistics	Criminalística
gas chromatography mass spectrometry (GC/MS)	cromatografía de gases acoplada a espectrómetro de masas
gauge (of a shotgun)	calibre de escopeta
gel electrophoresis	electroforesis en gel
genetic marker	identificador genético
genetic pattern	configuración genética
genital area	zona genital
genital injuries using the face of a clock	desgarros genitales según el cuadrante horario
give great store	darle enorme valor a
give off an odor	desprender un olor
glass container	envase de vidrio
glass fragment	trozo de cristal, vidrio
gloves	guantes
glow in the dark	que brilla en la oscuridad
goggles	gafas, anteojos protectores
gouge (n)	boquete
gouge (v)	abrir o hacer una ranura
graph (v)	graficar
graph paper	papel cuadriculado
graphology	grafología
gravel	grava
grime	mugre
grinding	pulido
grip	empuñadura, cacha
grip safety	seguro de la empuñadura
grooved bore	ánima rayada
grooves	estrías, rayas
gross weight	peso bruto
grouping	acopio
gruesome	horripilante, truculento

Criminalistics	Criminalística
GSR- gunshot residue	residuos del fulminato o de pólvora combustionada
gunpowder	pólvora
gunshot wound	herida de bala
gut	intuición
gynecological exam	examen ginecológico
hacksaw	sierra de arco
hair	pelo, cabello
hair cortex	córtex (m) del pelo
hair cuticle	cutícula del pelo
hair follicle	folículo piloso
hair medulla	canal central, médula del pelo
hair sample	muestra de cabello o pelo
hair spray	laca, fijador
half burned	semicalcinado
hammer	martillo
hammer (of a gun)	percutor (de un arma de fuego)
handgun	arma corta
handle (v)	manipular
handling	manipulación
handwriting analysis	grafología
handwriting expert	experto caligráfico
hanging	ahorcamiento
hard hat	casco
head area	región cefálica
heart attack	infarto, ataque al corazón
heat-seal	cerrar herméticamente
helical grooves	estriado helicoidal
hem	dobladillo
hematology	hematología
hematoma	hematoma

Criminalistics	Criminalística
hemin crystals	cristales de clorhidrato de hematina
hemoglobin	hemoglobina
hemorrhage	hemorragia
Henry System	Sistema Henry
high explosive	detonante, alto explosivo
high performance liquid chromatography (HPLC)	cromatografía líquida de alto rendimiento
high resolution scanner	escáner de alta definición
high speed reader	lectora de alta velocidad
high velocity pattern	proyección a gran velocidad
hinder	entorpecer
hinge	gozne, bisagra
hit the target	incidir en el blanco
hoax bomb device	bomba falsa
hold down	sujetar
hollow	cuenco
hollow point	de punta hueca
holograph	testamento ológrafo
holster	funda, pistolera
homemade bomb	explosivo casero
homicide	homicidio
human hair	pelo humano
hydrochloric acid	ácido clorhídrico
hydrogen peroxide	peróxido de hidrógeno
hymeneal quadrant	cuadrante himeneal
ice pick	punzón
ideal surface	superficie idónea
identifying mark	marca o señal de identificación
IED - improvised explosive device	aparato explosivo improvisado
igniter	encendedor

Criminalistics	Criminalística
imbed	incrustar
imbedded	incrustado
impact angle	ángulo de incidencia
imperceptible	impalpable
implant	implante
in relief	en relieve
incendiary device	aparato incendiario
indentation	hendidura
indented writing	marcas en papel por apoyo al escribir
index finger	dedo índice
indirect light	iluminación oblicua
individual characteristic	elemento identificador, característica singular
infrared light	rayos infrarrojos
injury	lesión
ink roller	rodillo
inked fingerprint card	dactilograma
inkjet printer	impresora inyección de tinta
inkpad	placa para la tinta, tampón
inside out	reverso
internal hemorrhaging	hemorragia interna
internal injury	lesión interna
intoxication	intoxicación
investigate	indagar
iodine	yodo
iodine fuming	vapores de yodo
IR light	luz infrarroja, rayos infrarrojos
iterations	repeticiones
it's a match	coinciden
it's not a match	no coinciden
jacket	camisa, coraza

Criminalistics	Criminalística
jacketed	encamisado, blindado
jackknife (n)	navaja
jagged	irregular
jar	frasco, envase
jimmy	palanqueta
Kastle-Meyer color test	reacción Kastle-Meyer
kinship	consanguinidad
knife	cuchillo
knife (v)	apuñalar
knifing	apuñalamiento
known document	documento de referencia o indubitado
known print	huella indubitada, huella conocida
lab coat	bata blanca
lab kit	maletín o estuche de trabajo
lab technician	técnico del laboratorio
label (n)	etiqueta, marbete
label (v)	etiquetar
labor-intensive	que requiere mucha mano de obra
laceration	laceración
lacquer	laca
lands	campos
laser beam	haz de láser
laser illumination of prints	láser revelador de huellas
laser printer	impresora láser
latent fingerprint	huella dactilar latente
layer	capa
lead (n)	plomo
leak proof container	recipiente hermético
left-handed	zurdo

Criminalistics	Criminalística
letter bomb	carta bomba
lever	palanca
lie detector	detector de mentiras
ligature	ligadura
lime	cal
litmus paper	papel tornasol
litmus test	prueba de acidez
live explosive	explosivo activo
lividity	lividez
livor mortis	livor mortis, lividez cadavérica
log book	cuaderno de bitácora
loop	presilla, lazo
loop pattern	dibujo de presillas
low explosive	deflagrante
lower extremities	extremidades inferiores
lubrication ring	anillo de lubricación
luminol	luminol
lump	grumo
machete	machete
machine gun	ametralladora
macroscopy	macroscopía
magazine	cargador, peine
magazine base	base del cargador
maggots	gusanos
magnetic powders	polvos magnéticos
magnifying glass	lupa
make	marca
makeshift	improvisado, provisional
manslaughter	homicidio sin premeditación
manufacturer	fabricante
mar	dañar, estropear

Criminalistics	Criminalística
margin note	acotación
mark (v)	señalar
mark evidence	marcar pruebas
mass spectrometer	espectrómetro de masas
match	concordar, coincidir
match closely	concuerdan con mucha exactitud
match rather closely	corresponden, concuerdan con bastante exactitud
material evidence	pruebas materiales
measuring tape	cinta métrica
medical examiner	médico forense
medical report	dictamen médico
metal sheet	lámina de metal
metallic dust	polvo metálico, limadura
methanol	metanol
methodology	metodología
microscope	microscopio
microscopy	microscopía
microspectrometer	microespectroscopio
microspectrophotometer	microespectroscopio
middle finger	dedo medio o cordial
misconception	idea falsa
misfire	tirar en falso, fallar
mishandle (v)	manejar con ineptitud
missing child	niño extraviado
mixing bowl	bol o tazón
model	modelo
modeling clay	arcilla
moisten	humedecer
mold (n)	moldeado, molde, vaciado
Molotov cocktail	cóctel Molotov

Criminalistics	Criminalística
momentum	velocidad, momento
monkey wrench	llave inglesa
morgue	tanatorio, depósito de cadáveres
morphology	morfología
mortal wound	lesión o herida mortal
motive	móvil
mouth lesion	lesión bucal
move an object	desplazar un objeto
mud	fango, lodo, barro
murder	homicidio
murder victim	interfecto, occiso
muzzle (of a gun)	boca
nail	clavo
neck is broken	desnucar, desnucada
needle	aguja
needle mark	puntura de inyección, pinchazo
needle tracks	huellas de aguja
net weight	peso neto
neutron activation analysis	análisis por activación de neutrones
nib track	surcos dejados por el bolígrafo
nick	muesca, hendidura
nick (v)	mellar
nightstick	porra
ninhydrin	ninhidrina
nitrate products	productos nitrados
nitric acid	ácido nítrico
nitrocellulose	nitrocelulosa
non-consensual	sin consentimiento
non-porous	no poroso
nose (of a bullet)	ojiva, punta

Criminalistics	Criminalística
nose configuration	perfil de la punta
nosebleed	hemorragia nasal
notation	anotación, apunte
notch (n)	mella, melladura
notebook	cuaderno o libreta
noteworthy characteristics	características sobresalientes
nucleotide	nucleótido
nunchuks	chacos
oblique lighting	luz oblicua, luz reflejada
obliterate	erradicar, borrar
obliteration	eliminación, erradicación
obliteration of serial number	erradicación del número de serie
official letter	oficio
on the order of 1 in 100,000	del orden de 1 en 100,000
on-site inspection report	acta de inspección ocular
ooze	supurar
ooze out from	rezumar de
origin	procedencia, foco
overdose	sobredosis
overhead projector	retroproyector
over-stamp (v)	regrabar
over-stamping	regrabado
pack	envasar
package (v)	embalar, empaquetar, envasar
packaging	embalaje
paint chip	raspado de pintura
paint scraping	raspadura de pintura
paint thinner	disolvente de pintura
palm	palma de la mano
palm print	huella palmar

Criminalistics	Criminalística
palpable	palpable
paper box	caja de cartón
papillary ridges	crestas papilares
paraffin	parafina
paraffin gauntlet test	prueba del guantelete
paraffin mold	molde de parafina
partial print	huella fragmentaria, huella parcial
particle	partícula
patch (v)	retocar
patchy	disparejo, a trozos
path	trayectoria, recorrido
pathologist	patólogo
pattern of injuries	el cuadro lesivo
paving stone	adoquín
paw print	huellas de pisadas animales
pedometer	podómetro
pellet gun	carabina de posta
pen pressure	fuerza de apoyo (de bolígrafo)
penetration	acceso carnal, penetración
penis	pene
penknife	cortaplumas
pent-up gases	gases acumulados
percussion cap	cápsula fulminante
perfectly sound	bien fundado
perineum	periné
perishable	perecedero
perpetrator	autor
petri dish	plato de laboratorio
petroleum distillates	solventes de hidrocarburos
phenolphthalein	fenolfateína
phenotype	fenotipo

Criminalistics	Criminalística
photocopy machine	(máquina) fotocopiadora
photograph	fotografía
photographic records	archivos fotográficos
photomicrography	fotomicrografía
physical evidence	pruebas físicas
physical exam	exámen físico
piercing instrument	instrumento perforante
pill box	pastillero
pin	alfiler
pinpoint	precisar, establecer con exactitud
pipe bomb	bomba de tubo
pipette	pipeta
pistol	pistola
pistol grip	puño de pistola, empuñadura
pitted	rugoso
place	lugar, ubicación
plain arch	arco plano
plain whorl	torbellino
plaster	escayola, yeso
plaster of paris	escayola
plastic bag	bolsa de plástico
plastic seal	tapa o tapón de plástico
plastic tape	cinta adhesiva
plastic tie	cierre de plástico
plasticine	plastilina
plumb line	plomada
plywood	madera terciada
point of origin (of a fire)	foco del incendio
points of identification	puntos característicos, minucias
poison pen letters	anónimo ponzoñoso

Criminalistics	Criminalística
poisoned	envenenado
poisoning	envenenamiento
police report	dictamen policial
polygraph	detector de mentiras
polymorphism	polimorfismo
pool of blood	charco de sangre
pore	poro
positively identify	categóricamente identificar
posterior surface	cara posterior
postmortem lividity	lividez cadavérica, livor mortis
potassium nitrate	nitrato de potasio
powder	talco
powder tattooing	tatuaje
precisely aligned	alineadas con exactitud
preserve	conservar, preservar, proteger
preserve evidence	conservar pruebas
presumptive test	prueba de orientación
primer	cebo, fulminante
print	huella, reseña
print processor	procesadora de huellas
print technician	técnico en huellas
probative elements	elementos probatorios
probative value	valor probatorio
process a crime scene	procesar el lugar de los hechos
process trace evidence	procesamiento de rastros
profile	perfil
projectile	proyectil, bala
prone position	en decúbito ventral o prono, boca abajo
propane	propano
propellant	propulsante
protect and preserve	proteger y preservar

Criminalistics	Criminalística
	técnicas de seguridad
protection techniques	técnicas de protección
pry marks	marcas de palanca
psychiatric exam	estudio psiquiátrico
pubic area	zona púbica
pubic hair	pelo del pubis
pull back	replegar
pull out	arrancar
pull out by the root (of the hair)	arrancado del bulbo de la raíz del pelo
pulmonary edema	edema pulmonar
pump action	de mecanismo de corredera
puncture mark	pinchazo
putrefaction	putrefacción
Q tip	bastoncillo de algodón, hisopo
questioned bullet	proyectil problema
questioned document	documento dubitado
radial loop	presilla interna o radial
radioactive isotopes	radioisótopos
radioactive probes	sondas radioactivas
range	alcance
ransack	revolver, saquear
ransom note	nota exigiendo un rescate
rape (n)	violación
rape (v)	violar
razor	navaja de afeitar
razor blade	hojilla (hoja) de afeitar
reagent	reactivo
recidivist	reincidente
recoil	culatazo, retroceso
record (n)	registro, constancia
red blood cells	glóbulos rojos

Criminalistics / Criminalística

Criminalistics	Criminalística
reference sample	muestra de referencia
registered mail	correo certificado
reliable	fehaciente
relief	relieve
remains	restos, residuos
resealable	que se puede volver a cerrar
resin	resina
resolution	definición
retail gun dealer	corredor de armas
reveal (v)	revenir
revolver	revólver
RH factor	factor RH
ribbon	cinta de tela
ricochet	rebote
ridge dot	punto
ridge island	ojal
ridges	crestas
ridges of the skin	las crestas de la piel
rifle	fusil, rifle
rifled bore	ánima rayada, ánima estriada
rifling	rayado, estriado
right side out	anverso
right-handed	diestro
rigidly set	fijado rígidamente
rigor mortis	rigidez cadavérica, rigor mortis
rim	reborde
rimfire ammunition	municiones de percussion periférica
ring finger	dedo anular
rip (v)	rasgar, romper
rough sketch	croquis
rough surface	superficie rugosa

Criminalistics	Criminalística
round (of fire)	balazo, tiro
round-nose (bullet)	de cabo redondeado, de punta ojival
rub against	rozar contra
rubber gloves	guantes de hule
rubber sole	suela de caucho
rubbing	fricción
rule out	descartar
ruler	regla
rummage	hurgar en
run over	atropellar
run a test	efectuar o llevar a cabo un análisis
rust	herrumbre
sadistic	sádico
safe insulation	aisladoras de caja fuerte
safeguard	resguardar
safekeeping	resguardo
safety helmet	casco protector
safety lever	llave de seguridad
saline solution	solución salina
sample population	población de muestra
Saturday night special	arma de baja calidad
saw (n)	sierra, serrucho
sawdust	serrín
sawed-off shotgun	escopeta recortada
scale reference	referencia de escala
scalp	cuero cabelludo
scalpel	bisturí
scar	cicatriz
scatter shot	perdigones
scope rings	anillos del visor

Criminalistics	Criminalística
scorching	quemadura
scrape (n)	excoriación, arañazo
scrape (v)	raspar
scraping	raspadura
scratch (n)	ralladura, arañazo
scratch (v)	arañar, rallar
scratch marks	arañazos, rasguños
screen wire	tela metálica
screwdriver	destornillador
seal (v)	sellar, precintar
seal the scene of a crime	cerrar y conservar el lugar de los hechos
seal with wax	lacrar
seal (v)	sellar
sealant	sellador
sealing wax	lacre
search (n)	búsqueda, registro
search and compare	búsqueda y confronte
sebaceous glands	glándulas sebáceas
second degree burns	quemaduras de segundo grado
second-guess	cuestionar a posteriori
secure (v)	resguardar, poner a seguro
secure the scene	acordonar o asegurar el lugar de los hechos
security (video) tape	cinta de la cámara de seguridad, cinta de vigilancia
security thread	hilo de seguridad
self defense	defensa propia
self-inflicted wound	lesión auto-infringida
semen	semen
semen stains	manchas de semen
semi-automatic rifle	fusil semiautomático

Criminalistics	Criminalística
semi-jacketed	semi encamisado
seminal acid phosphatase	fosfatasa ácida en el semen
separatory funnel	embudo separador
serial killer	asesino en serie
serial number	número de serie
serial number restoration	regeneración de marcas seriales
serology	serología
set (a cast)	fraguar
set on fire	prenderle fuego
severed limb	extremidad cortada
sex offender	delincuente sexual
shallow grave	tumba poco profunda
shard	fragmento, esquirla
shards of metal	esquirlas de metal
sharp instrument	instrumento punzante
sharp point	punta afilada
sharp weapon	arma cortante o punzante
shatter	hacer añicos o pedazos
shaving (n)	viruta
sheet of X ray film	placa de película de rayos X
shellac	laca
shield number	número de insignia
shim	cuña
shock wave injury	lesión por onda expansiva
shoe covers	cubre zapatos
shoe print	huella de pisada calzada
shot (of a shotgun) (n)	perdigones
shotgun	escopeta
shotgun shells	cartuchos de escopeta
shoulder weapon	arma de cañón largo
shrapnel	metralla

Criminalistics	Criminalística
sickle	hoz
side-by-side	yuxtapuesto
sides	costados
sift	tamizar
signs of struggle	señales de lucha
signs of violence	señales de violencia
silencer	silenciador
silicone rubber putty	masilla de silicona
silver nitrate	nitrato de plata
sketch (n)	croquis
	hacer un croquis, levantar un
sketch (v)	croquis
skull	cráneo
slant	inclinación
slash	rajar, acuchillar
sledgehammer	almádena
slide	portaobjetos
slide (of a pistol)	corredera
slight hematoma	hematoma circunscrito
slit throat	degollación
slow down	entorpecer
slug	balín
smear (n)	frotis
smear (v)	embadurnar de
smidgen	pizca
smokeless powder	pólvora sin humo
smooth bore	ánima lisa
smooth sketch (for court use)	plano
smudge ring	ahumamiento
sniper	francotirador
snub nose	de cañón chato

Criminalistics	Criminalística
soak (v)	impregnar, macerar
sodium carbonate	carbonato sódico
sodomy	sodomía
soft-point	de punta blanda
sole	suela
sole of shoe	suela del zapato
sole of the foot	planta del pie
soot	hollín
sound assumption	suposición lógica
sound spectrogram	audiograma
sound spectrograph	espectrógrafo acústico
spacing	espaciado
spark	chispa
spatter	salpicadura
spatula	espátula
special handling	manipulación segura
spectrogram	audiograma, espectrograma
spectrographic analysis	análisis espectrográfico
spectrometer	espectrómetro, espectroscopio
spectrophotometer	espectrofotómetro
spectroscope	espectroscopio, espectrómetro
spectroscopy	espectroscopía
speculum	espéculo
spent cartridge casing	casquillo (gastado)
sperm	esperma
spermatozoa	espermatozoide
spilled blood	sangre vertida
spit (n)	saliva
spit (v)	escupir
splint	tablilla
spot	mácula, mancha

Criminalistics	Criminalística
spray (v)	pulverizar, rociar
spray bottle	pulverizador
spray paint (v)	pintar con atomizador o pulverizador
spurt	brotar
sputum	esputo, saliva
stab wound	puñalada
stabbing	apuñalamiento
stain	mancha
stain (v)	manchar
stained	maculado, manchado
stamped	estampado
stampings	estampillados
standard procedure	procedimiento normal
state-of-the-art	de vanguardia
statute of limitations	ley de prescripción
stearic acid	ácido esteárico
steel pipe	tubo de acero
stereomicroscope	estéreomicroscopio
sterile saline solution	solución salina estéril
sterilizing equipment	equipo esterilizador
stick	palo
stippling	tatuaje
stool	taburete
stopper	tapa, tapón
straight razor	navaja barbera
strand of hair	hebra de cabello
strangulation	estrangulación
striation	estría
striking energy	fuerza de impacto
string	hilo
stroke	derrame cerebral

Criminalistics	Criminalística
struggle (n)	forcejeo
strychnine	estricnina
stun	aturdir
styrofoam	espuma de poliestireno
subdural hemorrhage	hematoma subdural
subject to decay	que puede sufrir descomposición
suffocation	asfixia
suicide	suicidio
sulphur	azufre
superficial cut	lesión incisa superficial
superglue	cola de contacto, súper cola
supine position	en decúbito dorsal, boca arriba
surface	soporte, superficie
surgical cap	gorro quirúrgico
surrounding area	lugares aledaños, alrededores
syringe	jeringa
swab	frotis
sweat	transpiración, sudor
sweat glands	glándulas sudoríparas
Swiss army knife	navaja de mil usos, navaja múltiple
switch	interruptor
switchblade	navaja de resorte
sword	espada
symmetrical	simétrico
symptom	síntoma
table knife	cuchillo de mesa
tadpole shape	en forma de renacuajo
tag (n)	etiqueta
tag (v)	etiquetar, ponerle una etiqueta
tamper	manipular

Criminalistics	Criminalística
tape (n)	cinta adhesiva
tape lift (v)	levantar con cinta adhesiva
tape recorder	grabadora
tar	alquitrán, chapopote
tarnished	deslustrado
tattooing	tatuaje
tearing	desgarro
tearing of the perineum	desgarro perineall
teeth marks	huellas de dientes
teflon coated bullets	balas revestidas de teflón
temperature	temperatura
ten finger print	(impresión) decadactilar
tented arch	arco tendido
test bullet	bala patrón
test fire	disparo de prueba, disparo experimental
test tube	tubo de ensayo
thick	espeso
thin-layer chromatography	cromatografía de capa fina
thoroughly check	verificar minuciosamente
thread	hilo
thumb	pulgar
tie down	atar
ties	amarras
time	hora
time fuse	temporizador
timeline	cronología
timing mechanism	temporizador
tip of finger	punta, yema del dedo
tips of the fingerprints	yemas de los dedos
tire iron	quita llantas
tire marks	marcas de llantas, huellas de

Criminalistics	Criminalística
	neumáticos
title history	documentación de titularidad
tomography	tomografía
toner	toner
tongue depressor	aplicador de madera
tool marks	marcas de herramientas
tooth marks	huellas de dientes
torn	roto
toxicology	toxicología
trace	rastro, indicio, vestigio
trace elements	elementos trazadores
trace evidence	pruebas de rastro
traces of blood	rastros sanguinolentos
traces of strangulation with a rope	signos de estrangulamiento con lazo
tracing	calcado
tracking dog	perro adiestrado, perro rastreador
tracks	huellas, rastros
trait	rasgo
trajectory	recorrido
trajectory rod	sedal, sonda acanalada
transverse	transversal
trauma to the head	trauma craneal
traumatic shock	shock traumático
trend	tendencia
trigger	gatillo, disparador
trigger guard	guardamonte
trigger handle	asa del gatillo
tripod	trípode
turpentine	trementina
tweezers	pinzas, tenacillas

Criminalistics	Criminalística
typed letter	carta mecanografiada
ulnar loop	presilla externa o lunar, presilla cubital
ulnar side	lado cubital
ultraviolet light	luz ultravioleta
ultraviolet spectroscope	espectrómetro infrarrojo
unburned particles	granulaciones incombustas
unchangeable	inmutable
underlying fracture	fractura subyacente
unique	singular, peculiar
unknown blunt object	un objeto contundente desconocido
unknown print	huella dubitada, huella desconocida
unpremeditated	impremeditado
upper extremities	extremidades superiores
UV light	luz ultravioleta
vacuum packed	envasado al vacío
vagina	vagina
vaginal cavity	cavidad vaginal
vaginal penetration	penetración vaginal
vaginal smear slide	frotis vaginal
vaginal walls	paredes vaginales
vapor	vapor
vaporize	pulverizar
variable	variante
varnish	barniz
vat	tanque, cuba, tina
velocity impact	velocidad de la proyección
vial	ampolleta, ampolla
vicinity, in the	sitios aledaños
video camera	cámara de video

Criminalistics	Criminalística
visual inspection	inspección ocular
voiceprint	audiograma
Vucetich System	Sistema Vucetich
vulva	vulva
vulva region	zona vulvar
wad cutter	cortador del taco
wadding	taco
walking stick	bastón
water mark	marca de agua
water soluble	soluble en agua
water tank	tanque de tiro
wax	cera
wax paper	papel parafinado
weather conditions	condiciones climáticas
well within the expected range of	encaja bien en la gama de resultados esperados
where residue is likely to be deposited	en las zonas mas frecuentes de maculación
white cloth	tela blanca
whorl	verticilo
whorl pattern	dibujo de verticilo
with a high degree of certainty	con un alto grado de certeza
wood pulp	pulpa de madera
wood shaving	viruta de madera
wood sliver	astilla
wooden splint	tablilla
Wood's lamp	aparato de luz de Wood
worn area	zona desgastada
wrapped	envuelto
wrapping	envoltorio
X ray diffraction unit	difractor de rayos X

Criminalistics	Criminalística
Y incision	incisión de Y
yaw	ladear
zip gun	arma de fuego casero

Criminalística

Criminalistics

abolladura	dent (n)
abollar	dent (v)
abrasivo	abrasive
abrir una ranura	gouge (v)
acabado	finish (n)
acceso carnal por via anterior	vaginal penetration
acceso carnal por via posterior	anal penetration
acelerante	accelerant
acetona	acetone
ácido	acid
ácido clorhídrico	hydrochloric acid
ácido esteárico	stearic acid
ácido nítrico	nitric acid
acopio	gathering, collection
acordonar	cordon off
acordonar el lugar de los hechos	secure the scene
acotación	margin note
acotar	annotate
acta de defunción	death certificate
acta de inspeccion ocular	on-site inspection report
acumulación de creosota	creosote build-up
ADN-ácido desoxirribonucleico	DNA-deoxyribonucleic acid
adoquín	cobblestone
adulterar	falsify
aglutinina	agglutinin
agua destilada	distilled water
aguja	needle
aguja percutora	firing pin
agujero de bala	bullet hole
ahogamiento	drowning
ahorcamiento	hanging

Criminalística	Criminalistics
ahumamiento	smudge ring, bullet wipe
aisladoras de cajas fuertes	safe insulation
alcance	range
alcohol etílico	ethyl alcohol
aleación	alloy
alelo	allele
alfiler	pin
alineadas con exactitud	precisely aligned
almádena	sledgehammer
alquitrán	tar
alrededores	surroundings
alto explosivo	high explosive
amalgama	filling (of a tooth)
amarras	ties
amartillar	cock (v)
ametralladora	machine gun
aminoácido	amino acid
ampolla	vial
ampolleta	vial
añadido	addition
análisis de salpicaduras de sangre	blood spatter analysis
análisis de sangre	blood analysis
análisis por activación de neutrones	neutron activation analysis
analizador de espectro óptico	emission spectrograph
analizar	analyze
ángulo de dirección	directionality angle
ángulo de incidencia	impact angle
anillo de lubricación	lubrication ring, cannelure ring
anillos de burbujas	bubble rings

Criminalística	Criminalistics
anillos del visor	scope rings
ánima	bore
ánima estriada	rifled or grooved bore
ánima lisa	smooth bore
ánima rayada	grooved bore
ano	anus
anónimo ponzoñoso	poison pen letter
anotación	notation
anteojos protectores	goggles
anticuerpos	antibodies
antígeno	antigen
antropometría	anthropometry
anverso	right side out
apagallamas	flash suppressor
aparato de detección electrostático	electrostatic detection apparatus
aparato de luz de Wood	Wood's lamp
aparato explosive improvisado	IED - improvised explosive device
aparato incendiario	incendiary device
aplicador de madera	tongue depressor
aporrear	bludgeon
apuñalada	stabbed
apuñalamiento	stabbing, knifing
apuñalar	knife, stab (v)
arañar	scratch (v)
arañazo	scratch, laceration
arcilla	modeling clay
arco	arch
arco plano	plain arch
arco tendido	tented arch
arcos	arches

Criminalística	Criminalistics
arma contundente	blunt weapon
arma corta	handgun
arma cortante	sharp weapon
arma de cañón largo	shoulder weapon
arma de fuego	firearm
arma de fuego casero	zip gun
arma punzante	sharp weapon
arrancar	pull out
arsénico	arsenic
arteria seccionada	breached artery
arteriosclerosis	arteriosclerosis
asa del gatillo	trigger handle
asesino en serie	serial killer
asfixia	asphyxia, soffocation
aspermia	aspermia
astilla	chip, wood sliver
astilla de pintura	paint chip
ataque salvaje	brutal attack
atar	tie down
atentado con bomba	bomb attack
atraso	backlog
atropellar	to be run over
audiograma	voiceprint, spectrogram
aumentar	enlarge, increase
autopsia	autopsy
autor	perpetrator
avancarga, de	front loading
avanzado estado de descomposición	advanced stage of decomposition
azufre	sulphur
bala patrón	test bullet

Criminalística — Criminalistics

Criminalística	Criminalistics
bala que no estalla	dud
balas revestidas de teflón	teflon coated bullets
balazo en la cabeza	bullet to the head
balazo	round, shot
balín	slug
balística	ballistics
ballesta	crossbow
bandeleta contusiva	contusion ring
barandilla	banister
bario	barium
barnis	varnish
barro	mud
base de adhesión	adhesive base
base de datos	data base
base del cargador	magazine base
bastón	walking stick
bastoncillo de algodón	Q tip
bata blanca	lab coat
bencidina	benzidine
bengala	flare
bien fundado	perfectly sound
bifurcación	bifurcation
bioquímica	biochemistry
bisagra	hinge
bisturí	scalpel
blindado	jacketed
boca (de un arma de fuego)	muzzle (of a firearm)
boca abajo	face down
boca arriba	face up
bol	mixing bowl
bola de fuego	fireball

Criminalística	Criminalistics
bolsa de plástico	plastic bag
bomba de tubo	pipe bomb
bomba falsa	hoax bomb device
boquete	gouge (n)
borde cortante	sharp edge
borde filoso	sharp point or edge
bordes irregulares	irregular edges
borrado por limado	filed off
borrados	erasures
borrar	obliterate, erase
botar	throw away, dump (v)
brilla en la oscuridad	glow in the dark
brotar	spurt, gush
brote arterial	arterial spurting/gushing
brújula	compass
búsqueda y confronte	search and compare
cabello	hair
cabo redondeado	round-nose
cacha	butt (of a firearm)
cadáver	cadaver
cadena de custodia	chain of custody
caja de cartón	cardboard box
cal	lime
calafateo	caulk
calcado	tracing
calcinado	charred, burnt
calibre	caliber
calibre de escopeta	gauge
callos	callus
cámara de gases	fuming cabinet
cámara de vaporización	fuming cabinet

Criminalística

Criminalistics

cámara de video	video camera
camisa (de una bala)	jacket (of a bullet)
campos (del cañón de un arma de fuego)	lands (of a gun barrel)
canal central (del pelo)	hair medula
cañón chato	snub nose
cañon de un arma de fuego	barrel of a gun
capa	layer
cápsula fulminante	detonator cap, percussion cap
cara posterior	posterior surface
carabina de aire comprimido	BB gun
carabina de posta	pellet gun
característica singular	individual characteristic
carbón	charcoal
carbonato sódico	sodium carbonate
carbonizado	charred
cargador	magazine
carta bomba	letter bomb
carta mecanografiada	typed letter
cartucho	cartridge
cartuchos de escopeta	shotgun shells
casco	safety helmet, hard hat
casquillo	casing
casquillo (gastados)	spent cartridge casing, brass
catalizador	catalyst
cavidad vaginal	vaginal cavity
cebo	primer
celofán	cellophane
cenizas	ashes
cera	wax

Criminalística	Criminalistics
cercar con sogas	cordon off
cerrar herméticamente	heat-seal
cerrar y conservar el lugar de los hechos	seal the scene of a crime
chacos	nunchuks
charco de sangre	pool of blood
chispa	spark
cianoacrilato	cyanoacrylate
cicatriz	scar
ciencia forense	forensic science
científico forense	criminalist
cierre de plástico	plastic tie, fastener
cifrar digitalmente	digitally encode
cinta adhesiva	tape
cinta de la cámara de seguridad	security tape
cinta de tela	ribbon
cinta de vigilancia	security tape
cinta industrial	duct tape
cinta métrica	measuring tape
citrato	citrate
clavo	nail
cloratos y nitrato de amonio	ammonium nitrate fuel oil (ANFO)
cloro	bleach
coágulos	clots
cóctel Molotov	Molotov cocktail
coinciden	it's a match
coincidir	match (v)
cola de contacto	superglue
colposcopio	colposcope
comando anti-bomba	bomb disposal unit
compás	compass

Criminalística	Criminalistics
cómplice	accomplice
con un alto grado de certeza	with a high degree of certainty
concordar	match
concuerdan con mucha exactitud	match closely
concuerdan con bastante exactitud	match rather closely
condiciones climáticas	weather conditions
conducta desviada	deviant behavior
configuración genética	genetic pattern
confrontación	comparison
congénito	congenital
congruente con	consistent with
consanguinidad	blood relationship
consecuente con	consistent with
conservar	preserve
conservar pruebas	preserve evidence
constancia	record
contaminante	contaminant
contaminar	contaminate
contorno	contour, shape
contusión aguda	acute contusion
contusiones	bruising
coraza (de una bala)	jacket (of a bullet)
cordel	cord
corredera	slide
corredor de armas	retail gun dealer
correo certificado	registered mail
correr	flow (v)
cortada	cut (n)
cortador de cajas	box cutter
cortador del taco	wad cutter

Criminalística

Criminalística	Criminalistics
cortapernos	bolt cutter
cortaplumas	penknife
corte transversal	cross section
córtex (m) del pelo	hair cortex
costados	sides
cotejo	comparison
cotejo dactilar	fingerprint comparison
cotejo de armas de fuego	firearms comparison
cráneo	skull
crestas	ridges
crestas de la piel	ridges of the skin
crestas papilares	friction ridges
criminalística	criminalistics
criminalística de campo	field investigation
criptografía	cryptography
cristales de clorhidrato de hematina	hemin crystals
cromatografía	chromatography
cromatografía de capa fina	thin-layer chromatography
cromatografía de gases	gas chromatography
cromatografía de gases acoplada a espectrómetro de masas	gas chromatography mass spectrometry (GC/MS)
cromatografía líquida de alto rendimiento	high performance liquid chromatography (HPLC)
cronología	timeline
croquis	sketch, rough sketch
croquis a escala	drawing to scale
cuaderno de bitácora	log book
cuaderno	notebook
cuadrante himeneal	hymeneal quadrant

Criminalística	Criminalistics
cuadro lesivo	pattern of injuries
cuarto oscuro	darkroom
cuba	vat
cubierta exterior del pelo	hair cuticle
cubre zapatos	shoe covers
cuchillo	knife
cuchillo de mesa	table knife
cuchillo de combate	commando knife
cuenco	hollow
cuero cabelludo	scalp
cuerpo presenta calcinado en un 80% de la superficie corporal	there are burns over 80 % of the body
cuestionar a posteriori	second-guess
culata	butt
culatazo	recoil
cultivo	culture
cuña	shim
cutícula del pelo	hair cuticle
dactilograma	inked fingerprint card
daga	dagger
dañar	mar, damage
darle enorme valor a	give great store to
de manera concluyente	conclusively
decámetro	decameter
decapitar	decapitate
decolorante	bleaching agent
decúbito dorsal, en	in a supine position
decúbito ventral o prono	in a prone position
dedo anular	ring finger
dedo cordial	middle finger
dedo índice	index finger

Criminalística	Criminalistics
dedo medio	middle finger
defensa propia	self defense
definición	resolution, definition
deflagrante	low explosive
deformación	defacement, distortion
degollación	slit throat
degollado	slit throat
degradar	degrade
del orden de 1 en 100,000	on the order of 1 in 100K
delincuente sexual	sex offender
deltas	deltas
dentadura postiza	dentures
depósito de cadáveres	morgue
depósito de pruebas	evidence locker
depósito grasoso sudoríparo	body oil
depresiones	depressions
dermis	dermis
derrame cerebral	stroke
desangramiento	exsanguination
desangrar	bleed out
descarnar	remove the flesh from, bare
descartar	rule out, reject
descomposición	decay, decomposition
desecar	dry out
desfigurar	deface, disfigure
desgarro	tearing
desgarros genitales según el cuadrante horario	genital injuries using the face of a clock
desgarro perineal	tearing of the perineum
deslustrado	tarnished
desmembración	dismemberment

Criminalística	Criminalistics
desmembrar	dismember
desnucamiento	broken neck
despejar el lugar	clear the area
desperfecto	flaw
desplazar	displace, move
desplazar un objeto	move an object
desprender un olor	give off an odor
desprendimiento	detachment, release
destornillador	screwdriver
desviación	divergence
detector de mentiras	lie detector, polygraph
detonador	detonator
detonante	high explosive
dibujo de huellas dactilares	fingerprint pattern
dibujo de arcos	arch pattern
dibujo de presillas	loop pattern
dibujo de verticilo	whorl pattern
dibujo forense	forensic art
dictamen médico	medical report
diestro	right-handed
difenilamina	diphenylamine
difractor de rayos X	X ray diffraction unit
dirección de la proyección	directionality
disecar	dissect
disolvente de pintura	paint thinner
disparejo	patchy, uneven
disparo de prueba	test fire
disparo experimental	test firing
disposición	disposition
doblez	crimp
documentación de titularidad	title history

Criminalística	Criminalistics
documento adulterado	damaged document, counterfeit document
documento dubitado	questioned document
documento falsificado	forged or counterfeit document
documento indubitado	known document
droga de la violación	date rape drug
edema	edema
edema pulmonar	pulmonary edema
editor de gráficos rasterizados	digital imaging enhancement
efectuar análisis	run tests
ejemplar	exemplar
electrocución	electrocution
electroforesis en gel	gel electrophoresis
elemento "testigo"	control sample
elemento identificador	accidental or individual characteristic
elementos probatorios	probative elements
elementos trazadores	trace elements
eliminación	obliteration, elimination
embadurnar de	smear with
embalaje	packaging
embalar	package (v)
embudo separador	separatory funnel
empaste	filling
empírico	empirical
empuñadura	grip
empuñadura delantera	foregrip
en forma de renacuajo	tadpole shape
en grandes lineas	broadly

Criminalística

Criminalistics

en las zonas mas frecuentes de maculación	where residue is likely to be deposited
en relieve	embossing, in relief
encaja bien en la gama de resultados esperados	falls well within the expected range
encamisado	jacketed
encendedor	igniter
encolado	binder
encriptar	incript, digitally encode
encubridor	accessory after the fact
engarce	crimp
engarzado a presión	crimp sealed
enlazar	bind
enmascarar	deface
enmasillado	caulk
ensangrentado	bloodstained
entomólogo	entomologist
entrada forzada	forced entry
envasado al vacío	vacuum packed
envasar	package, bottle, pack(v)
envase de vidrio	glass container
envase para pruebas	evidence container
envenenado	poisoned
envenenamiento	poisoning
envenenamiento por monóxido de carbono	carbon monoxide poisoning
envoltorio	wrapping
envoltura (de bala)	bullet jacket
epidermis	epidermis
equimosis (moretón)	ecchymosis (bruise)
equipo esterilizador	sterilizing equipment

Criminalística	Criminalistics
erradicación	obliteration
erradicación del número de serie	obliteration of serial number
erradicar	obliterate
escáner de alta definición	high resolution scanner
escayola	plaster
escombros	rubble, debris
escopeta	shotgun
escopeta recortada	sawed-off shotgun
escrito disfrazado	disguised handwriting
escrito imitado	disguised handwriting
escupir	spit (v)
espaciado	spacing
espada	sword
espada de dos filos	double-edged sword
espátula	spatula
espectrofotómetro	spectrophotometer
espectrógrafo acústico	sound spectrograph
espectrograma	spectrogram
espectrómetro	spectrometer
espectrómetro de masas	mass spectrometer
espectroscopía	spectroscopy
espectroscopio	spectroscope
espéculo	speculum
espéculo anal	anal speculum
esperma	sperm
espermatozoide	spermatozoa
espiral	whorl
espoleta de retardo	delayed fuse
espuma de poliestireno	styrofoam
esputo	sputum, spit
esquirlas de metal	shards of metal

Criminalística	Criminalistics
establecer con exactitud	pinpoint
estampado	cast or stamped
estampillados	stampings
estéreomicroscopio	stereomicroscope
estrangulación	strangulation, strangled
estrechadura	crimp
estría	rifling, striation, groove
estriado helicoidal	helical grooves, checkering
estricnina	strychnine
estuche de trabajo	lab kit
estudio psiquiátrico	psychiatric exam
etiqueta	tag, label (n)
etiquetar	label (v)
examen anatómico	anatomical exam,
examen ginecológico	gynecological exam
exámen somero	cursory examination
exámen superficial	cursory examination
excoriación	abrasion
expectador	bystander
experto caligráfico	handwriting expert
exploración física	physical exam
explosivo activo	live explosive
explosivo casero	homemade bomb
expulsor	ejector
extremidades inferiores	lower extremities
extremidades superiores	upper extremities
exumación	disinterment
eyaculación	ejaculation
fabricación	manufacture
fabricante	manufacturer
factor RH	RH factor

Criminalística · Criminalistics

Criminalística	Criminalistics
fallecido	deceased
falsificar	falsify, forge
falso positivo	false positive
fango	mud
fecha	date
fechar	date (v)
fehaciente	reliable
fenolftaleína	phenolphthalein
fenotipo	phenotype
fetiche	fetish
fetichista	fetishist
fibra	fiber
fibra de tela	cloth fiber
fibra textil	cloth fiber
ficha dactilar	fingerprint card
fijado rígidamente	rigidly set
fijar	affix, set
finado	deceased
firma facsímil	facsimile signature
flecha	arrow
flúidos corporales	bodily fluids
fluorescer	fluoresce
fluoroscopio	fluoroscope
foco del incendio	point of origin (of a fire)
folículo piloso	hair follicle
forcejeo	struggle (n)
fórceps	forceps
fosa	cavity
fosfatasa ácida	acid phosphatase
fosfatasa ácida en el semen	seminal acid phosphatase
fotocopiadora	photocopy machine

Criminalística	Criminalistics
fotografía	photograph
fotografía ampliada	enlarged photograph
fotomicrografía	photomicrography
fractura	fracture
fractura subyacente	underlying fracture
fragmento	shard, fragment
fraguar	set (as in a cast)
francotirador	sniper
frasco	bottle, jar
frotis	smear
frotis vaginal	vaginal smear
fuente	source, font
fuente de luz alternativa	alternate light source
fuerza de apoyo (de un bolígrafo)	pen pressure
fuerza de impacto	striking energy, force of impact
fulminante	primer
funda	casing, holster
fusil	rifle
fusil automático	automatic rifle
fusil semiautomático	semi-automatic rifle
gafas protectoras	goggles
gas butano	butane gas
gases	fumes, gases
gases acumulados	pent-up gases
gatillo	trigger
glándulas sebáceas	sebaceous glands
glándulas sudoríparas	sweat or eccrine glands,
glóbulos rojos	red blood cells
golpe contuso	blunt force trauma

Criminalística

golpiza	beating
gorro quirúrgico	surgical cap
gota de sangre	blood drop
gotas	drops
gotero	dropper, eye dropper
gozne	hinge
grabadora	tape recorder
graficar	graph (v)
gráfico	chart (n)
gráfico de barras	bar chart
grafología	handwriting analysis
granulaciones incombustas	unburned particles
grava	gravel
grieta	crevice
grumo	lump
grupo sanguíneo	blood type
guantes	gloves
guantes de hule	rubber gloves
guantes desechables	disposable gloves
guardamonte	trigger guard
gusanos	maggots
hacer un croquis	draw a sketch
hacer una ranura	gouge (v)
hacha	ax
hallazgos	findings
haz de laser	laser beam
hebra de cabello	strand of hair
hematologia	hematology
hematología forense	forensic hematology
hematoma (m)	hematoma
hematoma circunscrito	slight hematoma

Criminalistics

Criminalística	Criminalistics
hematoma subdural	subdural hemorrhage
hemoglobina	hemoglobin
hemorragia	bleeding, hemorrhage
hemorragia aguda	acute hemorrhage
hemorragia interna	internal hemorrhaging
hemorragia nasal	nosebleed
hendidura	Indentation, impression
hendiduras de percutor	firing pin indentations
herida a bocajarro	contact wound
herida a quemarropa	contact wound
herida de arma blanca	stab wound
herida de bala	gunshot wound
herida de muerte	fatal wound
herrumbre	rust
hilo	string, thread
hilo de seguridad	security thread
hirsuto	bristly
hisopo	Q tip, swab
hoja de afeitar	razor blade
hojilla de afeitar	razor blade
hojuela	flake
hollín	soot
homicidio	murder, homicide
homicidio sin premeditación	manslaughter
hora	time
horquilla	ends of ridges
horripilante	gruesome
hoz	sickle
huella	print
huella dactilar latente	latent fingerprint
huella de pisada	footprint

Criminalística	Criminalistics
huella de pisada calzada	shoe print
huella de pisada descalza	barefoot print
huella desconocida	unknown print
huella digital	fingerprint
huella digital latente	latent fingerprint
huella dubitada	unknown print
huella fragmentaria	partial print
huella indubitada	known print
huella modelo	known print
huella palmar	palm print
huella parcial	partial print
huellas	tracks, prints
huellas de aguja	needle tracks
huellas de dientes	teeth marks
huellas de herramientas	tool marks
huellas de neumáticos	tire marks
huellas de pisadas animales	animal prints or tracks
humedecer	moisten
hurgar en	rummage
iluminación oblicua	indirect light
impalpable	imperceptible
implante	implant
implante de seno	breast implant
implante en las nalgas	buttocks implant
impregnar	soak
impresión dactilar	fingerprint
impresion dactilar dubitada	unknown print
impresión decadactilar	ten finger print
impresión nítida	clean print
impresora inyección de tinta	inkjet printer
impresora láser	laser printer

Criminalística	Criminalistics
impresora matriz de puntos	dot matrix printer
improvisado	makeshift, improvised
incendio doloso	arson
incidir en el blanco	hit the target
incisión de Y	Y incision
inclinación	slant
incrustado	embedded
incrustar	embed
indagar	investigate
infarto	heart attack
inflamable	flammable
inmutable	unchangeable
instrumento cortante	sharp instrument
instrumento perforante	piercing instrument
instrumento punzante	sharp instrument
interfecto	murder victim
interruptor	switch
intoxicación	intoxication
irregular	jagged
jeringa	syringe
juntas de baldosines	tile joints
laca	lacquer, shellac, hair spray
laceración	laceration
lacrar	seal with wax
lacre	sealing wax
ladear	yaw
laguna de sangre	pool of blood
lámina de metal	metal sheet
láser revelador de huellas	laser illumination of prints
lazos	loops

Criminalística	Criminalistics
lazos de bolsa central	central pocket loop
lazos gemelos	double loop whorls
lectora de alta velocidad	high-speed reader
legía	bleach
lesión	injury
lesión auto-infringida	self-inflicted wound
lesión bucal	mouth lesion
lesión incisa superficial	superficial cut
lesión interna	internal injury
lesión mortal	fatal injury
lesión mortal	mortal wound or injury
lesión por onda expansiva	shock wave injury
lesiones de defensa	defensive wounds
letra cursiva	cursive writing
letra de mano	cursive or handwriting
letra tergiversada	disguised handwriting
levantar con cinta adhesiva	tape lift (v)
ley de prescripción	statute of limitations
ligadura	ligature
lijado	filing
lima	file (n)
limar	file (v)
linterna	flashlight
líquido de embalsamar	embalming fluid
lividez	lividity
lividez cadavérica	postmortem lividity
livor mortis	livor mortis
llama	flame
llave de boca	crescent wrench
llave de seguridad	safety lever
llave inglesa	monkey wrench

Criminalística	Criminalistics
lodo	mud
luminol	luminol
lupa	magnifying glass
luz de bengala	flares
luz infrarroja	IR light
luz oblicua	oblique lighting
luz reflejada	oblique lighting
luz ultravioleta	ultra-violet light
macerar	soak
machete	machete
macroscopía	macroscopy
mácula	spot
madera terciada	plywood
maletín de trabajo	lab kit
mamas	breasts
mancha	stain
mancha de sangre	bloodstain
manchado	stained
manchar	stain
manchas de sangre	bloodstain patterns
manchas de semen	semen stains
manchas por proyección	cast-off pattern
manejar con ineptitud	mishandle
manipulación	handling
manipulación segura	special handling
manipular	tamper, handle
manoplas	brass knuckles
manos ensangrentadas	bloodstained hands
marbete	label (n)
marca	make
marca de agua	watermark

Criminalística

marcación serial	serial number
marcador genético	genetic marker
marcapasos	pacemaker
marcas de dientes	bite marks, teethmarks
marcas de filigranas	water marks
marcas de herramientas	tool marks
marcas de la recámara	breech marks
marcas de llantas	tire marks
marcas de neumáticos	tire marks
marcas de palanca	pry marks
marcas del bloque de cierre	breechblock marks
marcas del espaldón	breechblock marks
marcas del extractor	extractor marks
marcas distintivas	distinctive marks
marcas en papel por apoyo al escribir	indented writing
martillo	hammer
masilla de silicona	silicone rubber putty
matada a golpes	beaten to death
material encefálico	brain matter
matraz	flask
mecanismo de corredera	pump action
mechero Bunsen	Bunsen burner
médico forense	medical examiner
médula (del pelo)	hair medula
mellar	nick, chip (v)
mellas de percutor	firing pin indentations
meñique	baby finger
metanol	methanol
metodología	methodology
métodos para deshacerse de	disposal methods
metralla	shrapnel

Criminalística

Criminalistics

	microspectrophotometer
microespectroscopio	microspectrometer
microfotografía	microphotography
microscopía	microscopy
microscopio	microscope
microscopio de comparación	comparison microscope
minucias	points of identification
modelo	model
molde	mold, cast (n)
molde de parafina	paraffin mold
moldeado	mold, cast (n)
moldeo	casting
momento	momentum
mono	overall, coverall
monóxido de carbono	carbon monoxide
mordaza	gag
mordedura	bite mark
moretón	contusion, bruise
morfología	morphology
mota	fleck
motosierra	chain saw
movimiento del proyectil	flight pattern
muerte accidental	accidental death
muesca	nick
muestra de cabello	hair sample
muestra de control	control sample
muestra de referencia	reference sample
muestra de sangre	blood sample
muestra testigo	control sample
mugre	grime
mugre de las uñas	fingernail scrapings

Criminalística	Criminalistics
municiones de percusión central	center fire ammunition
municiones de percusión periférica	rimfire ammunition
navaja	jackknife
navaja barbera	straight razor
navaja de afeitar	razor
navaja de mil usos	Swiss army knife
navaja de resorte	switchblade
navaja múltiple	Swiss army knife
necropsia	autopsy
ninhidrina	ninhydrin
niño extraviado	missing child
nitrato de amonio y combustible derivado del petróleo	ammonium nitrate fuel oil (ANFO)
nitrato de plata	silver nitrate
nitrato de potasio	potassium nitrate
nitrocelulosa	nitrocellulose
no coinciden	it's not a match
no poroso	non-porous
no se alinean	do not line up
nota exigiendo un rescate	ransom note
nucleótido	nucleotide
nudilleras	brass knuckles
número de expediente	file number
número de insignia	shield number
número de serie	serial number
número del caso	case number
objeto contundente desconocido	unknown blunt object
observación directa	direct observation
obtener un resultado fidedigno	arrive at a reliable result
obtener, preservar y valorar	collect, preserve, evaluate

Criminalística	Criminalistics
occiso	murder victim
ocultamiento	concealment
oficio	official letter
ojal	enclosure or ridge island, eyelet
ojiva	nose
onda explosiva	blast
orificio de entrada	entry wound
orificio de salida	exit wound
overol	coverall, overall
palanca	lever, crowbar
palanca de armar	cocking piece
palanqueta	jimmy
palma de la mano	palm
palo	stick
palpable	palpable
papel (de) tornasol	litmus paper
papel carbón	carbon paper
papel celofán	cellophane
papel cuadriculado	graph paper
papel filtro	filter paper
papel impermeable	waterproof paper
papel parafinado	wax paper
papel secante	blotting paper
papel tornasol	litmus paper
parafina	paraffin
paredes vaginales	vaginal walls
paro cardíaco,	cardiac arrest
partícula	particle
pastillero	pill box
patólogo	pathologist
patrón de desgaste	wear pattern

Criminalística

Criminalistics

patrón de uso	wear pattern
peine (de un arma de fuego)	clip (of a firearm)
película pancromática	color film
peligro biológico	biohazard
pelo	hair
pelo animal	animal hair
pelo del pubis	pubic hair
pelo humano	human hair
pene	penis
penetración anorrectal	anal penetration
penetración vaginal	vaginal penetration
percutor	hammer, firing pin
perdigones	scatter shot
perecedero	perishable
perenne	constant
perfil de la punta	nose configuration
periné	perineum
periodicidad	frequency
perito en balística	ballistics expert
perito en dactiloscopia	fingerprint expert
peróxido de hidrógeno	hydrogen peroxide
perro adiestrado	tracking dog
perro rastreador	tracking dog
peso bruto	gross weight
peso neto	net weight
pesquisa	investigation
picaporte de puerta	door handle
piel descamada	flaking (of the skin)
pincel	brush
pincelada	brushstroke
pinchaso	puncture, needle mark

Criminalística	Criminalistics
pintar con atomizador	spray paint (v)
pinzas	tweezers
pipeta	pipette
pista	clue
pistola	pistol
pistolera	holster
pizca	smidge, smidgen
placa de película de rayos x	sheet of X ray film
placa para la tinta	inkpad
plano	smooth sketch (for use in court)
planta del pie	sole of the foot
plastilina	plasticine
plato de laboratorio	petri dish
plomada	plumb line
plomo	lead
plumas	feathers
población de muestra	sample population
podadera	pruning shears
podómetro	pedometer
polimorfismo	polymorphism
polvo	powder
polvo magnético	magnetic fingerprint powder
polvo metálico	metallic dust
pólvora	gunpowder
pólvora sin humo	smokeless powder
polvos magnéticos	magnetic powders
poner a seguro	secure (v)
poro	pore
porra	billy club, nightstick
portaobjetos	slide

Criminalística

Criminalística	Criminalistics
posibilidad	chances, possibility
precintar	seal
precisar	pinpoint
presilla	fastener, loop
presilla cubital	ulnar loop
presilla externa o lunar	ulnar loop
presilla interna o radial	radial loop
procedencia	origin, source
procedimiento normal	standard procedure
procesadora de huellas	print processor
procesamiento de rastros	process trace evidence
procesar el lugar de los hechos	process a crime scene
productos nitrados	nitrate products
profundidad	depth
propano	propane
propiedad grupo específico	class characteristic
propinar una paliza	beat up
propulsante	propellant
protector facial	face shield
proteger y preservar	protect and preserve
proyección a gran velocidad	high velocity pattern
proyectil	bullet, projectile
proyectil problema	questioned bullet
prueba de acidez	litmus test
prueba de orientación	presumptive test
prueba del guantelete	dermal nitrate test, paraffin gauntlet test
prueba irrebatible	irrefutable evidence
pruebas físicas	physical evidence
pruebas materiales	material evidence
puedan sufrir descomposición	subject to decay
pulgar	thumb

Criminalística	Criminalistics
pulido	grinding
pulpa de madera	wood pulp
pulverizador	spray bottle
pulverizar	vaporize, spray
puñal	dagger
puño de pistola	pistol grip
puños	cuffs
punta (de bala)	nose (of bullet)
punta afilada	sharp point
punta blanda	soft-point
punta hueca	hollow point
punta ojival	round-nose
punto (de huellal)	ridge dot (of print)
punto de mira	front site
puntos característicos	points of identification
puntos de crestas papilares	ends of ridges
puntura de inyección	needle mark
punzón	ice pick
putrefacción	putrefaction
quemadura	scorching, burn
quemaduras de primer grado	first degree burns
quemaduras de segundo grado	second degree burns
química forense	forensic chemistry
quitallantas	tire iron
radioisótopos	radioactive isotopes
ralladura	scratch, scrape (n)
rasgado	torn
rasgo	trait
rasguños	scratch marks
raspado de pintura	paint chip
raspadura	scraping

Criminalística	Criminalistics
raspadura de pintura	paint scraping
raspar	scrape
rastro	trace
rastro indiciario	trace evidence
rastro indumentario	clothes fiber
rastro único	accidental characteristic
rastro vestimenta	clothes fiber
rastros	trace, tracks
rastros de violencia	signs of violence
rastros sanguinolentos	traces of blood
rayado	rifling
rayadura	scratch
rayas	grooves, striations
rayos infrarrojos	infrared light
reacción Kastle-Meyer	Kastle-Meyer color test
reacción microcristalográfica	crystal test
reactivo	reagent
reactivo químico	etching agent
reborde	rim
rebote	ricochet
recabar datos	collect data
recámara	breech, chamber
recipiente de vidrio	glass container
recipiente hermético	leak proof container
recogedor	dust pan
recolectar	collect
recopilación de pruebas	collection of evidence
recorrido	trajectory, path
referencia de escala	scale reference
	serial number
regeneración de marcas seriales	restoration
region cefálica	head area

Criminalística

Criminalistics

registro	record, search (n)
registro de reserva	backup record
registro minucioso	careful search
regla	ruler
regrabado	over-stamping
regrabar	over-stamp
reguero de sangre	blood trail
reincidente	recidivist
relieve	relief
repeticiones	iterations
replegar	pull back
replegar los colgajos	pull back the skin
requiere mucha mano de obra	labor-intensive
resguardar	safeguard
resguardo	safekeeping
residuos	remains, residue
residuos de pólvora combustionada	GSR - gunshot residue
residuos debajo de las uñas	fingernail scrapings
residuos del fulminato	GSR- gunshot residue
resina	resin
restos	remains
restos de explosivo	bomb remains
retocar	patch
retrato compuesto	composite sketch
retrocarga, de	breech loading
retroceso	recoil
revelado de huellas dactilares	fingerprint development
reveladores de huellas	fingerprint powders
revelar	dust, develop (v)
revelar una huella	dust a print
revelar película	develop film

Criminalística	Criminalistics
revenir	reveal (v)
reverso	inside out
revólver	revolver
rezumar de	exude, ooze out from
rifle	rifle
rigidez cadavérica	rigor mortis
rociar	spray (v)
rodillo	ink roller
romper	rip, break
roto	torn
rotular	label (v)
rozar contra	rub against
rugoso	bumpy, pitted
sádico	sadist
saliva	saliva, spit
salpicadura	fleck, spatter
salpicadura de sangre	blood spatter
sangre coagulada	clotted blood
sangre de drago	dragon's blood
sangre desecada	dried blood
saquear	ransack
se puede volver a cerrar	resealable
secado al aire	air-dried
seco	desiccated, dried out
sedal	trajectory rod
seguro de la empuñadura	grip safety
sellador	sealant
sellar	seal, stamp
semen	semen
semi encamisado	semi-jacketed
semicalcinado	half burned

Criminalística	Criminalistics
señalar	mark (v)
señales de forcejeo	signs of struggle
señales de violencia	signs of violence
señas particulares	distinguishing marks
senos	breasts
serología	serology
serrín	sawdust
serrucho	saw
shock traumático	traumatic shock
sierra	saw
sierra de arco	hacksaw
signos de estrangulamiento con lazo	traces of strangulation with a rope
signos de quemadura	burn marks
silenciador	silencer
simétrico	symmetrical
simulador	faker
sin consentimiento	non-consensual
síntoma	symptom
sistema de almacenamiento de datos	data storage system
sistema Henry	Henry system
sistema Vucetich	Vucetich system
sitios aledaños	in the vicinity
situacion engorrosa	awkward situation
sobre de celofán	cellophane envelope
sobredosis	overdose
sobredosis de drogas	drug overdose
sobres	envelopes
sodomía	sodomy
solapa	flap
soluble en agua	water soluble

Criminalística

solución buffer	buffer solution
solución salina	saline solution
solución salina estéril	sterile saline solution
solventes de hidrocarburos	petroleum distillates
sonda	catheter
sonda acanalada	trajectory rod
sondas radioactivas	radioactive probes
soporte	surface, support, holder
soporte liso	flat surface
sudor	sweat
suela	sole
suela claveteada	cleated sole
suela de caucho	rubber sole
suela del zapato	sole of shoe
suicidio	suicide
sujetar	hold down, hold
sulfato de difenilamina	diphenylamine sulfonate
superficie anterior	anterior surface
superficie idónea	ideal surface
superficie rugosa	rough surface
suposición lógica	sound assumption
supurar	ooze
surcos	furrows
surcos dejados por el bolígrafo	nib tracks
tablilla	wooden splint
tablilla con sujetapapeles	clipboard
taburete	stool
taco	wadding
talco	powder
tambor (de revólver)	cylinder (of a revolver)
tamizar	sift, filter (v)

Criminalística	Criminalistics
tampón (para tinta)	inkpad
tanatorio	morgue
tanque	vat
tanque de tiro	water tank or trap
tapa	stopper
tapa de plástico	plastic seal
tapón	stopper
tarjeta de colores opuestos	card of contrasting colors
tatuaje	tattooing, stippling
técnicas de informática forense	computer enhancement
técnico del laboratorio	lab technician
técnico de huellas digitales	print technician
tela blanca	white cloth
tela metálica	screen wire
temperatura	temperature
temporizador	time fuse, timing mechanism
tenacillas	tweezers
tenazas	forceps
tendencia	trend
testigo mudo (cadáver)	dumb evidence (corpse)
tiempo trascurrido	elapsed time
tinta	dye
tipificacion del ADN	DNA typing
tirar	dump (v)
tirar en falso	misfire
tizas de colores	colored chalk
toner	toner
toner electrostático	electrostatic copy toner
torbellino	plain whorl
toxicología	toxicology

Criminalística	Criminalistics
transpiración	sweat
transversal	transverse
trauma craneal	trauma to the head
trauma ocasionado por fuerza contundente	blunt force trauma
trayectoria	path
trazas de violencia	signs of violence
trementina	turpentine
trípode	tripod
trozo de cristal	glass fragment
trozo de ropa	clothes fragment
trozo de vidrio	glass fragment
truculento	gruesome
tubo de acero	steel pipe
tubo de ensayo	test tube
tumba poco profunda	shallow grave
ubicación	place, location
vaciado	cast (n)
vaciar	cast, empty (v)
vagina	vagina
vainilla	cartridge casing
valorar la prueba	evaluate the evidence
vanguardia, de	state-of-the-art
vapor	vapor
vapores de yodo	iodine fuming
variante	variable
vaso de precipitados	beaker
velocidad	speed
velocidad de la proyección	velocity impact
verificar minuciosamente	thoroughly check
verticilo	whorl

Criminalística	Criminalistics
verticilo accidental	accidental whorl
verticilos de bolsa central	central pocket loop whorls
verticilos gemelos	double loop whorls
vestigio	trace
via de acceso	path of entry
via de huida	escape route
violación	rape (n)
violar	rape (v)
viruta	shaving
viruta de madera	wood shaving
visor facial	face shield
vulva	vulva
yema del dedo	fingertip
yeso	plaster, plaster of paris
yodo	iodine
yuxtapuesto	side-by-side
zona desgastada	worn area
zona genital	genital area
zona púbica	pubic area
zona vulvar	vulva region
zurdo	left-handed

Abbreviations & Systems	Abreviaciones y Sistemas
ACE-V - analysis, comparison, evaluation and verification	análisis, cotejo, evaluación y verificación
AFTE- Association of Firearms and Tool Mark Examiners	Asociación de Examinadores de Armas de Fuego y Marcas de Herramientas
ASCLD-American Society of Crime Lab Directors	Sociedad Americana de Directores de Laboratorios de Criminalística
ATF- Bureau of Alcohol, Tobacco, Firearms and Explosives	Agencia de Alcohol, Tabaco, Armas de Fuego y Explosivos
CFR- Code of Federal Regulations	Código de Reglamentos Federales
CODIS -Combined DNA Index system	Sistema combinado de índices de ADN
DEA-Drug Enforcement Administration	Agencia Antidrogas, Administración de Drogas y Narcóticos
DNA -deoxyribonucleic acid	ADN - ácido desoxirribonucleico
ESDA-Electrostatic detection apparatus	Aparato de detección electrostático
FBI-Federal Bureau of Investigation	Oficina Federal de Investigación
IABPA-International Association of Bloodstain Pattern Analysts	Asociación Internacional de los Analistas del Patrón de la Mancha de Sangre
IBIS-Integrated Ballistic Identification System	Sistema Integrado de Formación de Imágenes de Balística

Abbreviations & Systems	Abreviaciones y Sistemas
INTERPOL-International Criminal Police Organization	Organización Internacional de la Policía Criminal
KM Test-Kastle-Meyer color test	Reacción Kastle-Meyer
Locard´s Exchange Principle	Teoría de (intercambio de) Locard
NAA-Neutron Activation Analysis	AAN-Análisis por Activación de Neutrones
NCIC-National Crime Information Center	Centro Nacional de Información Criminal
NRA-National Rifle Association	Asociación Nacional del Rifle
PCR-polymerase chain reaction	Reacción en cadena de la polimerasa
PDQ- paint data query	Base de Datos de Muestras de Pintura
PMI-post mortem interval	Intervalo post mortem
RFLP-Restriction fragment length polymorphism testing	Análisis del polimorfismo de restricción de longitud de fragmentos
SAEK - sexual assault evidence kit	Kit de atención a víctimas de agresión sexual
SNP-single nucleotide polymorphism (pronounced snip)	Poliformismo de nucleótido único
STR- short tandem repeats	Microsatélites
TMDT-Trace Metal Detection Technique	Técnica de Detección de Rastros de Metal

Abbreviations & Systems

Abreviaciones y Sistemas

UPIS- U.S. Postal
Inspection Service

Servicio Federal (EEUU)
de Inspección Postal

VICAP-Violent Criminal
Apprehension Program

Programa de detención
de criminales violentos

Bibliography

Beavan, Colin. Fingerprints. Hyperion, New York, 2001.

Bell, Suzanne, PhD. Encyclopedia of Forensic Science. Facts on File, Inc., New York, 2008.

Connors, Edward, Thomas Lundregan, Neal Miller, Tom McEwen. Convicted by Juries, Exonerated by Science: Case Studies in the Use of DNA Evidence to Establish Innocence After Trial. U.S. Department of Justice, National Institute of Justice, Gaithersburg, Feb. 1999.

Dowling, Jerry L. Criminal Investigation. Harcourt Brace Jovanovich, Inc., New York, 1979.

Fisher, Barry A.J., Arne Svensson, and Otto Wendel. Techniques of Crime Scene Investigation. Isevier Science Publishing Co., Inc., New York, 1987.

Fletcher, Connie. Every Contact Leaves a Trace. St. Martin's Press, New York, 2006.

Kvitko, Luis Alberto. La Violación. Editorial Trillas, S.A de C.V.,México, 2004.

Lee, Henry C., Ph D and Frank Tirnady. Blood Evidence- How DNA is Revolutionizing the Way We Solve Crimes. Perseus Publishing, Cambridge, 2003.

Bibliography –cont'd

Manzanera, Luis Rodríguez. Criminología Clínica. Editorial Porrúa, México, 2005.

Mikkelson, Holly. The Interpreter's Companion/PDF. ACEBO, Spreckels, 2001.

Moreno González, L. Rafael, Coordinador. Antología de la Investigación Criminalística. Instituto Nacional de Ciencias Penales, México, 2003

Nickell, Joe and John F. Fischer. Crime Science: Methods of Forensic Detection. The University Press of Kentucky, Lexington, 1999.

Rademaker, Mario Popoli. Los Aportes de la Criminalística en la Fase Preparatoria del Proceso Penal Venezolano. Vadell Hermanos Editores, Caracas, 2007.

Reyes Calderón, Jose Adolfo. Tratado de Criminalística. Cardenas Velasco Editores, S.A de C. V. México, 2005.

Waggoner, Kim, ed. Handbook of Forensic Services. An FBI Laboratory Publication, Quantico, 2007.

Order Form

<u>C</u>riminalistics for <u>S</u>panish-English <u>I</u>nterpreters

Place orders by sending an email to:
<u>csimillikan@gmail.com</u> with the following information:

Name:_____

Address:_____

_____

City: _____

State: _____ Zip Code_____

Email address

(required)_____

Sales Tax:

Please add 9.25 % for books shipped to California addresses.

Shipping:
First Class postage: $2.45 for one book; add $2.00 for each additional book.

Payment: Go to <u>www.paypal.com</u> and make payment to account "CSIMillikan."

Price $ 24.95 X _____ = _____

California Tax: _____

Shipping   _____

TOTAL TO BE PAID: _____

Order Form

<u>C</u>riminalistics for <u>S</u>panish-English Interpreters

Place orders by sending an email to:
<u>csimillikan@gmail.com</u> with the following information:

Name:_____

Address:_____

_____

City: _____

State: _____ Zip Code_____

Email address

(required)_____

Sales Tax:

Please add 9.25 % for books shipped to California addresses.

Shipping:
First Class postage: $2.45 for one book; add $2.00 for each additional book.

Payment: Go to <u>www.paypal.com</u> and make payment to account "CSIMillikan."

Price $ 24.95 X _____ = _____

California Tax: _____

Shipping   _____

TOTAL TO BE PAID: _____

.

pulmonary embolism
insurance carrier
anti-clot medication
preserve the claim